PROTESTANT-CATHOLIC
RELATIONS IN AMERICA

PROTESTANT-CATHOLIC RELATIONS IN AMERICA

World War I through Vatican II

LEROND CURRY

The University Press of Kentucky

ISBN: 0-8131-1265-6

Library of Congress Catalog Card Number: 79-183352

Copyright © 1972 by The University Press of Kentucky

A statewide cooperative scholarly publishing agency
serving Berea College, Centre College of Kentucky,
Eastern Kentucky University, Kentucky State College,
Morehead State University, Murray State University,
University of Kentucky, University of Louisville,
and Western Kentucky University.

Editorial and Sales Offices: Lexington, Kentucky 40506

To all
who have made
this book possible

Contents

Preface

The impact of Protestant-Roman Catholic interaction is too strong for the student of religion, history, or sociology to ignore or for the person in everyday life to evade. Because each of these major traditions of Christianity has profoundly affected the other the influence of either of them is at root the influence of both. Since the Reformation, Protestantism and Catholicism have often reacted against one another, often emulated one another, and often secretly—sometimes openly—admired one another. But they have never escaped one another. Relations between the two, while varying, are ever present.

In America these relations are particularly significant. For one thing this nation has a deep-rooted religious consciousness, reaching to its earliest settlers. Whatever individual Americans may feel about the importance of religion in their own lives, Americans as a whole recognize its vital role in the development of their society. For another, America is one of the few nations of the world whose Protestant heritage antedates its Catholic heritage. Even in lands where the Reformation was strongest there was a preexisting Catholic structure. But in most of the United States the earliest ecclesiastical roots were planted by Protestants. This has given interconfessional relationships in America a special coloring. Even so, Roman Catholicism finally became such a strong minority group in the country that its impact on the majority has often equaled the majority's impact on it. This has made Protestant-Catholic interaction in the United States especially intense.

In the history of Protestant-Catholic relations in America, World War I is especially important. It was the first truly global conflict the young nation had experienced. It made Americans increasingly self-conscious, and among large numbers a new nativism rose to challenge anything which it felt smacked of foreign power—including the Roman Pope. At the same time the war was a catalyst for the growth of Roman Catholic influence in America. It brought about the establishment of a National Catholic War Council in 1917, and shortly after the war American Catholics expanded this council into a permanent National Catholic Welfare Conference. Furthermore, as is the case with war generally, World War I brought on a renewed interest in religion. One sign of this was a church building boom during the decade which followed. Another sign was a fundamentalist-modernist doctrinal controversy among American Protestants which intensified following the war. All of these factors, once combined, increased the intensity of Protestant-Catholic interaction.

The subsequent history of Protestant-Catholic interaction in America has been marked by various phases, but at no time in the post World War I era has there been a lack of concern on the part of either religious establishment for its standing in relation to the other. Interfaith relations have been and still are ever present concerns. These concerns touch not only the organized church but also politics and society in general. The story of Protestant-Catholic relations, therefore, is a story which needs telling.

A number of volumes and articles have been published on various parts of the story of Protestant-Catholic relations in America since World War I, but to my knowledge there has been no general presentation of the overall story. It is for the purpose of making such a presentation that this volume is offered. Because detailed accounts are available of more confined phases of this story—for example the presidential campaigns of Al Smith and John Fitzgerald Kennedy—I have not attempted here to make an elaborate presentation of each phase. To have done so would have made this volume bulky and pedestrian. Rather, I have attempted to sift through the masses of primary and secondary materials pertaining to

Protestant-Catholic interaction in America since World War I and to relate here the highlights and central issues. Because of my own research I would be among the first to acknowledge that there are many cases and instances which offer exceptions to the general trends, but I am willing to stand by my contention that the story I have told in this volume is the story of the chief trends in Protestant-Catholic relations in America as they have developed in the past five to six decades. It is the story of the most widespread and influential patterns of interfaith behavior. This volume, then, is intended both as a synthesis of presently existing knowledge and as an analysis of some of the underlying factors in the broad story of Protestant-Catholic relations in post World War I America which have not been previously presented. It is my sincere hope that this volume will be useful to teacher and student and to clergyman and layman—in short, to any readers who are concerned with and interested in the affairs of religion and society.

Whatever shortcomings there are in this volume are of my doing; whatever contributions there are are the results of much guidance and encouragement by others. If I were to acknowledge all those to whom I am indebted for this project it would take many pages just to name them. Some of my greatest encouragement has come from friends who in informal conversations have expressed genuine interest in what I was doing and from colleagues in the field of religious studies and others in the fields of history and sociology who have deemed this study worthy of attention. Valuable insights have come from numerous people with whom I have corresponded or conversed during the course of my investigations, some of whom play key roles in the story presented in this volume. A special word of appreciation goes to Professor Maurice M. Vance of Florida State University whose careful attention to my research a few years ago has constantly inspired me to continue on my own. Finally, but by no means least, I acknowledge the encouragement of my wife, who by becoming my wife while this manuscript was in preparation gave me a vote of confidence seldom experienced by a writer.

I.

Protestant Adjustment to Catholic Growth: 1917-1939

Through the years prior to World War I Protestants and Roman Catholics in America were building up to a full-scale conflict. It was not the first time in this country that conflict was the rule, but it was a unique time in several ways.

Primarily, the early 1900s were years in which a Protestant-oriented America was trying to adjust to a rapidly growing Roman Catholicism in its midst. Although not really understanding its reactions in a theological framework, much of Protestant America feared its ecclesiastical counterpart precisely because it was both Roman and Catholic. Protestants feared its Roman roots because this smacked of an identifiable foreign influence in America. Terms such as "Romanism" and "the Roman church" came into increasing use in private conversations and public statements. Typical of the latter were the references to Al Smith, the Catholic nominated by the Democratic party for president in 1928, as a "rum-soaked Romanist."[1] The isolationist sentiment in America after World War I added to this fear. Since the Papacy is located in a foreign country, many an American undoubtedly felt that too much Papal influence in the United States would lead the nation into a dreaded "entangling alliance." The harsh experiences of the war just over caused a type of paranoia among some, which demanded that no further encroachments of this Italian figure be allowed among the people of America.

There were fears of the Roman church's "catholicity" also. Like any established group which feels some of its influence being lost to newcomers, many members of the Protestant establishment of the early twentieth century grew nervous. They knew that the church of Rome had a history of rapid growth, both in numbers and influence, almost everywhere it had taken root. In the United States this growth was occurring with amazing steadiness. During the last fifty years of the nineteenth century the Catholic population in America had increased from under 2 million to over 10 million. By World War I it was above 17 million.[2] Added to this was the fact that converts to Catholicism in the United States numbered 500,000 in the first two decades of the twentieth century alone, and this was over 40 percent more than the number of converts in the last three decades prior to that.[3] When in 1908 Pope Pius X declared that the United States was no longer a mission territory, Catholicism gained an even greater image of having unprecedented strength in America.[4]

There were other factors creating tensions as well. One of these was urbanization. As people moved to the cities they were thrown closer together both at home and at work. And since it is much easier to get the man out of his early environment than it is to get that environment out of the man, people who had grown up believing myths about the religiously unfamiliar found themselves fearful of what their Protestant or Catholic associates might really be up to. The proximity of people of a different religious orientation was a new experience for many of both faiths, especially Protestants who had migrated from the farms and Catholics who had immigrated from abroad. The novelty created anxiety in many from both groups, an anxiety which often expressed itself at best in clumsy interaction. Even in modern times a canon of the Washington National Cathedral who himself had developed strong interfaith contacts testified that the main difference he experienced in interfaith patterns in America from that of his native Ireland was that in the United States there was "social contact with Catholic laymen."[5]

At the same time, the less urbanized areas of the country fostered their own strong religious animosities. There were several causes of this. One was the common suspicion of that which is unfamiliar. And, in spite of the rapid Catholic growth, in many parts of the country, especially in the rural South, there were people whose personal contacts with Roman Catholics were quite limited and sometimes almost nil.[6] This suspicion with the unfamiliar lay behind much of the anti-Catholic sentiment in the more sparsely populated Protestant areas in the country.

There seems to have been, as well, a rural suspicion of urban areas in general behind those religious conflicts. This was one of the most subtle aspects of anti-Catholicism during the period of World War I. The majority of Roman Catholics lived in the cities. Since by the time of World War I many of the rural areas were losing young people to the cities, those that remained on farms and in smaller towns took a dim view of many things in urban society. In the religious life of this urban society were more and more Catholics. For some, therefore, their anti-Catholicism had anti-city overtones.

A further factor in the strengthening of anti-Catholic sentiment was a new wave of immigration which hit the shores of America in the decade prior to 1917. From 1907 until the outbreak of the war more than 650,000 people a year entered this country, with those from southern and eastern Europe far outnumbering the rest.[7] These immigrants lived primarily in the cities, hence increasing the rural Protestant suspicion of urban life which, of course, would include a distaste for the religion of these unfamiliar people from foreign soil. Furthermore, not only were these people different in their names and cultural patterns, but many of them were willing to work in the labor market at a much lower wage. The threat of being cut out of one's job was itself enough to cause consternation among workers already here. Consequently, many of these workers were hostile to anything that had to do with these immigrants. The fact that the immigrants were Roman Catholic made Catholicism guilty by association. The Catholic immigrants represented a powerful economic threat to large segments of the American labor force; therefore, their religion had to be discouraged and maybe they would go home.[8]

It would be wrong to assume, however, that the religious suspicions were all one-sided. Catholics in America, most of whom had come more recently out of European settings than most American Protestants, recalled more clearly some of the religious animosities of the Old World. The Catholics in America apparently saw in their Protestant neighbors reminders of their long-standing adversaries in Europe. Battle-worn Irishmen, for example, had been walling themselves off from their Protestant neighbors since the beginning of their immigration during the first half of the nineteenth century. Furthermore, for a century, Catholics in America had tended to segregate themselves in their schools. As a result, they too were subject to some deep-seated anxieties.

It is evident that the causes of Protestant-Catholic tensions in America by World War I were deep and complicated. It is doubtful that people who held anti-Catholic or anti-Protestant feelings knew completely why they did, and this no doubt caused even further stress. The Protestant of anti-Catholic bent not only disliked Roman Catholicism for reasons he could explain, but his distaste was increased because in his anti-Catholicism he, and consequently his own religious life, became even more of a puzzle to himself. Much the same was true with the American Catholic in his relations with Protestantism.

One thing is quite evident, however. The religious conflicts in the minds of most Americans of this period were not basically theological. They concerned, instead, the pocketbook, the neighborhood, the job, and city hall. Nor did the war change this. Rather, the war further complicated the social and political contexts in which religious differences were an issue.

It seemed at first that the entrance of the United States into World War I might lessen the internal religious strife in the country. People of divergent and even hostile persuasions have a way of getting together in face of a common threat, and so it was in 1917 and 1918. It mattered little who was defending the country as long as the country was being defended. In fact, James Cardinal Gibbons, one of America's foremost Catholic leaders, was commended by former President Theodore Roosevelt for his leadership during the war and was called by the former chief executive "the most respected, and venerated, and useful citizen in our country."[9] Furthermore, much of the welfare work of the armed forces was handled jointly by the Knights of Columbus, the Salvation Army, the Young Men's and Young Women's Christian Associations, and the Jewish Welfare Board. These various Catholic, Protestant, and Jewish organizations shared an active concern for the well-being of those directly affected in adverse ways by the war effort.[10]

But for the majority of people the war was not viewed as an opportunity to insure domestic tranquillity. It was simply something to get over as quickly as possible. Not only this, but the very goal of the war as seen by so many, the goal of making "the world safe for democracy," was viewed by some in such a way as to increase rather than decrease religious tensions. To many Americans this goal meant precisely "to make America safe." This in turn led many to conclude that nothing short of "one hundred percent Americanism" could be accepted of anyone who lived in the United States.

After World War I the slogan "return to normalcy," a slogan used by Warren Harding in his campaign for the presidency in 1920, captured the minds of many Americans. Though Harding himself did not conduct his campaign on the basis of anti-Catholicism, his election on a platform of "normalcy" was undoubtedly sufficient evidence in the minds of some who were predisposed to anti-Catholic sentiment that the nation had issued a mandate against the growing strength of the Roman Catholic church in America. For after all, people with anti-Catholic biases could reason, "normalcy" meant returning to whatever had been the American social order in former days, and since the early days of American history a decided Protestant majority had been "normal" in the country.

It was the new nativism of the postwar period coupled with the growing Roman Catholicism in the country that gave rise to a period of open conflict following the war. Those with a prevailing nativist ideology could not dismiss the fact that Roman Catholicism had a foreign leader. To the nativist's mind the Catholic's allegiance to a Pope in Rome ran counter to the ideal of "one hundred percent Americanism."[11]

Foremost among the expressions of nativism in the early postwar years was the revival of the Ku Klux Klan. In 1915 a southern rural salesman named William J. Simmons began the movement, naming it after the defunct Ku Klux Klan of Reconstruction days, and appointed himself "Imperial Wizard" of the organization.[12] A big boost for the hooded order came, however, in 1920, when two experienced publicity agents, Edward Y. Clarke and Mrs. Elizabeth Tyler, joined forces with Simmons. One year later there were Klan chapters in forty-five states, and the organization, with its fervor no doubt diminishing its statistical accuracy, claimed to be enlisting one thousand members a day.[13] The nationwide scope of the Klan of the 1920s made it quite different from the KKK of Reconstruction days when the hooded order was confined largely to the South.

John Higham, a student of American nativism of this period, suggests that Protestant fundamentalism was among the forces feeding the Klan.[14] It is worthy of note that American Protestantism in the postwar period was embroiled in a full-scale fundamentalist-modernist controversy in theological circles. As this controversy spread out to the nontheologically oriented, both camps grew in fervor and took up causes not directly related to the original issues. This seems to have been especially true of fundamentalism. Not only was it a body of doctrines, but for many of its adherents it became a full-scale social and political attitude.

There is not enough evidence to conclude that fundamentalism itself gave rise in any major degree to the Klan. It does seem likely, however, that some of the same forces were present to shape both, and because of this the Klan tended to appear more closely akin to Protestant fundamentalism than to any other religious movement. For one thing, both of these groups had a definite concern for orthodoxy—fundamentalism for absolute Biblical literalism, the Klan for "one hundred percent Americanism." This made it easier for some fundamentalists to feel drawn to the Klan than for people whose general outlook was not geared so highly to the spirit of orthodoxy. Furthermore, since Catholicism contained an extra-Biblical authoritative tradition culminating in the Papacy, fundamentalism had less difficulty sympathizing with the KKK's anti-Papal themes.

The Klan did utilize the methods of religious crusades to a great extent. This was done both to capture the public mind and to convince itself of the value of its existence. In this way it appealed to the religious drives of many of the same people to whom fundamentalism in its most rampant forms appeared. Each local chapter of the Klan had a chaplain who opened the meetings with a prayer. Altars were erected at meeting sites, and flaming crosses became well-known signs of Klan presence. The hooded order modified familiar hymns and used them as Klan songs, and, frequently, Klansmen would parade in full regalia into the midst of a Protestant Sunday service and give the minister a donation.[15]

The rise of the Ku Klux Klan, however, demonstrates most vividly that the anti-Catholic attitudes of Americans in the period following World War I were, like those of the days preceding it, primarily political. Simmons's successor as Imperial Wizard of the Klan, Hiram Wesley Evans, a Dallas dentist, stated that "the real objection to Romanism in America is not that it is a religion . . . but that it is a church in politics."[16] In order to avoid the accusation that the Klan was mixing politics and religion, Evans also stated that the hooded order represented "no ecclesiastical organization or sacerdotal hierarchy."[17]

The political orientation of the KKK is borne out by the fact that very few Klan statements about the Catholic church were doctrinal. Rather, they were aimed by means of a whispering campaign to play on the fears of those who were concerned for America's security following World War I, and of those who could not easily adjust to the growth of Catholicism in the country. Sometimes the claims became downright preposterous. There were tales of rifles buried beneath Catholic churches at the birth of each Catholic boy in anticipation of the day when the Roman church would revolt against the United States government. There were stories of secret drills by the Knights of Columbus, of priests who seduced women at confession, and most of all, of plans by the Pope to seize control of America. Klansmen could not seem to get together, however, on where the Pope was going to set up headquarters. Especially prominent in Indiana was a rumor that a "million dollar palace" was being built for the Pope in Washington, D. C., and that the Vatican was about to be moved to that city.[18] Governor Sidney J. Catts of Florida, with Klan blessing, went up and down the state warning citizens that the Pope planned to invade Florida and move the Vatican there.[19]

It was fear of the new and unfamiliar that caused these stories to be widely accepted. People who had had little contact with Catholics were often hard-put to know how to take this rapidly growing phenomenon in their country. The less well-informed of these people were easy prey for the scare tactics which the Klan used. Not the least among the reasons for these fears' taking root was the fact that priests and nuns of the Catholic church were identifiable by dress. This made them appear all the more militaristic to some Americans who, because of the recent world war, associated almost any kind of uniform with a military organization. The cassocks and habits of the priests and nuns also ran counter to the Protestant idea that a clergyman should be just another person and not set apart by ecclesiastical dress. There were some who felt that this concept of clergymen was a democratic idea *per se* and hence necessary in a democracy. Consequently, Catholic garb offended them just that much more. The fact that the Klan itself was uniformed by use of sheets no doubt accentuated the idea of warring forces. It probably aided the Klan's acceptance in some areas, as well, by making the masked organization appear as an army of loyal Americans, dressed in white, ready to oppose the black-garbed leaders of the conspiring Papal forces.

The Klan took its politically oriented anti-Catholicism into numerous political arenas. In the Democratic primary race in Atlanta in 1922, the Klan-supported councilman Walter Sims, who was opposed by organized Catholic efforts, won.[20] In the same year in Texas the Klan-endorsed Earl B. Mayfield won the Democratic nomination for United States senator in a race in which Catholicism was the dominant issue.[21] Most significant was the Klan's successful attempt at blocking the presidential nomination of Al Smith, the Roman Catholic governor of New York, at the 1924 Democratic national convention.[22]

The anti-Catholicism of the Klan during these years cannot be seen as simply a secondary emphasis. It seems to have surpassed even the anti-Negro outlook of the order.[23] Even though the Klan's heaviest concentration was in the South, where there was the largest Negro population, the state with the largest Klan membership in the 1920s was Indiana, which was estimated to have up to 700,000 people on Klan rolls.[24] Ohio and Texas were next, with around 400,000 Klansmen in each state.[25] It is noteworthy that the Klan grew strong in several states where the Catholic population far outnumbered the Negro population. Reasons for the strength of anti-Catholicism as a KKK emphasis in relation to the anti-Negro emphases lie once again in the phenomenon of unfamiliarity. Though the black man still was a stranger to the white man in the early 1920s, nevertheless the black man had been around for quite some time. Catholicism was newer and in some ways, therefore, more perplexing. Furthermore, the rapidity of Catholic growth in America was much greater than that of America's black population. There had been no widespread Negro influx into America since the end of the slave trade by act of Congress in 1808. Hence, whereas among blacks there was for the most part natural increase only, among Catholics there was both natural increase—itself quite significant because of the Catholic dogma prohibiting birth control—and the increase of the new immigration as well.

The Klan certainly did not go unopposed during these years. Members of the Catholic hierarchy in America readily denounced it, and in 1922, at the height of KKK political strength, the Knights of Columbus organized an anti-Klan campaign.[26] Several states, led by Iowa, Minnesota, and Michigan, passed laws in the early 1920s forbidding masked organizations.[27]

Sometimes there was violence. Herrin, Illinois, in the mid-1920s became the scene of several fatal shootings of both Protestants and Catholics.[28] Lafayette, Louisiana, saw bloodshed as the result of the publications of the names of charter members of the Klan in that area, and the Catholic hostility there became so high that their bishop, the Reverend Jules B. Jeanmard, publicly called for Catholics to refrain from wreaking "a cheap revenge upon the Klan."[29] In Carnegie, Pennsylvania, in August 1923, an illegally held Klan parade caused a riot which resulted in the death of one Klansman and a series of legal procedures which dragged on for five years until a judge declared that the Klan by virtue of its lawlessness had no status in court.[30] In Lilly, Pennsylvania, eight months later the "bloodiest Klan riot in the order's history from 1915 to 1928" left four people dead and twenty-nine rioters, twenty-five of whom were KKK members, indicted for murder. Twenty-eight of these were convicted on charges of unlawful assemblage and affray and received two-year prison sentences.[31]

The Ku Klux Klan also met opposition from some responsible Protestant sources. Though not mentioning the Klan by name, the Administrative Council of the Federal Council of Churches released the following statement in 1922:

The Administrative Council of the Federal Council of the Churches of Christ in America records its strong conviction that the recent rise of organizations whose members are masked, oath-bound, and unknown, and whose activities have the effect of arousing religious prejudice and racial antipathies is fraught with grave consequences to the Church and to society at large. Any organization whose activities tend to set class against class or race against race is consistent neither with the ideals of the churches nor with true patriotism, however vigorous or sincere may be its professions of religion and Americanism. . . .
The Administrative Committee of the Federal Council of the Churches is opposed to any movement which overrides the processes of law and order, and which tends to complicate and make more

difficult the work of cooperation between the various political, racial, and religious groups in the Republic. No such movements have the right to speak in the name of Protestantism and the churches are urged to exert every influence to check their spread.[32]

The Protestant press for the most part condemned the movement.[33]

It was not, therefore, Protestantism as an ecclesiastical movement that ran rampant with the nativism of the Klan variety. It was, however, sometimes difficult for Catholics to see this. They heard the Klan's cries more clearly than they did Protestant ecclesiastical denunciations of the hooded order. There is little in the Catholic periodical literature of the early 1920s to indicate that Catholics took much note of what the more responsible members of Protestant circles were saying. An editorial in the *Catholic World* of December 1923 implied that the majority of Protestants in America at the time were of the Klan variety.[34] It was more difficult for Catholics to separate politics and religion than it was for many non-Catholics. Thus, Catholics tended to see the KKK as religious opponents in spite of statements, even of the Klan, to the contrary. It tended to increase the defensiveness of American Catholics, also, for in defending themselves socially and politically they were defending their total identity, which, for them, included their ecclesiastical doctrines and practices. Through all of this, American Catholics tended to become as one writer has suggested, "as clannish as the Klan," [35] and consequently the years of the Klan were years which saw an increased separation on the part of the two largest religious establishments in America. What could have been a very ripe occasion for religious leaders in both groups to work together against a common enemy of lawlessness and bigotry was bypassed. Protestants bypassed it because even the mainline groups were uneasy about the growing Catholic influence in the country. Catholics bypassed it because they failed to distinguish adequately between American ecclesiastical Protestantism and American nativism.

By the mid-1920s the strength of the Ku Klux Klan was in decline. This was due not so much to opposition to the Klan as to the fact that the general public had grown weary of so much overt hostility. Because the masked order depended upon this method it lost its ability to sustain support.

But the cause of anti-Catholicism was far from lost. Hardly had the ballots been counted in the 1924 presidential election when the name of Al Smith began to appear more prominently as a contender for the 1928 Democratic nomination. This was simply further proof to many Protestants that the Catholics intended to control the government. Anti-Catholic propaganda presses were operating widely by 1926, and barbed comments were heard from influential sources—for example, the statement of Methodist Bishop Adna Leonard of Buffalo that "no Governor can kiss the papal ring and get within gunshot of the White House."[36] (Smith was reputed to have performed this ritual before Cardinal Bonzano when the latter visited the United States.) Even for this Methodist bishop it was not doctrinal implications of the ritual that seemed to bother him but rather the simple fact that a man who would perform such strange and bizarre acts could be so powerful politically. The bishop was determined that America would "remain Protestant."[37]

The question of Smith's Catholicism gained publicity as much, if not more, in the secular press than in ecclesiastical journals and circles, further demonstration of how widespread America's response to Catholic growth had become. Most prominent was an exchange of letters in the April and May issues of the *Atlantic Monthly* in 1927, between Smith and Charles C. Marshall, a New York lawyer versed in canon law. Marshall's letter appeared first. It reprimanded Smith for having neglected to address himself publicly to the question of his Roman Catholicism and its compatibility to the American Constitution. The lawyer asserted that the primary problem lay in the Catholic church's doctrine of the two powers, ecclesiastical and state, which at times made the church feel supreme over the state and which demanded of any conscientious Roman Catholic that he accept this view. Then came Marshall's pointed question to his governor:

Citizens who waver in your support would ask whether as a Roman Catholic you accept the authoritative teaching of the Roman Catholic Church that in case of contradiction, making it impossible for the jurisdiction of the Church and that of the State to agree, the jurisdiction of the Church shall prevail; whether as a statesman, you accept the teaching of the Supreme Court of the United States that, in matters of religious practices which in the opinion of the State are inconsistent with its peace and safety, the jurisdiction of the State shall prevail; and if you accept both teachings, how will you reconcile them?[38]

The unsung figure in this exchange was Ellery Sedgwick, editor of the *Atlantic Monthly*. Both his wife and son testified that Sedgwick was an enthusiastic supporter of Al Smith and felt strongly that religion was a highly improper issue for a presidential campaign.[39] It seems to have been his feeling that publishing a letter like Marshall's and then a reply from Smith would help eliminate the issue before the campaign really got underway. In the next issue of his periodical the editor himself wrote that it was "an historic incident for the country and for the Church" and asked rhetorically, "Is the principle of religious tolerance universal and complete, which every schoolboy has repeated for one hundred and fifty years mere platitudinous vaporing?"[40]

Al Smith was not enthusiastic about Sedgwick's idea of a public statement. When the *Atlantic Monthly* editor first sent him the proof sheets of Marshall's letter, the New York governor stated that he would not dignify the issue with a reply to Marshall. Sedgwick then called upon Teresa FitzPatrick, a loyal Roman Catholic on the *Atlantic Monthly* staff, to try to persuade Smith to change his mind. Miss FitzPatrick succeeded when she appealed to Governor Smith on the basis of the *Atlantic Monthly*'s influential subscribers and the opportunity Smith had to blot out "erroneous conclusions based on bigotry."[41]

By then the entire nation was so caught up in the question of Smith's Catholicism, a fact Smith never realized completely, that special care had to be taken to guard the manuscript containing the governor's reply. Sedgwick sent Miss FitzPatrick to pick up the governor's answer personally, and she did so, carrying it to the *Atlantic Monthly* office on a midnight train from New York to Boston. The efforts at protecting the manuscript were in vain, however, for a reporter from the *Boston Post* prevailed on the nightwatchman at the press where the *Atlantic Monthly* was already printing the reply to give him a copy of the pages which contained the governor's statement. The statement appeared the next day in the *Boston Post*, and the *Atlantic Monthly* editor quickly sued the Boston newspaper for infringement of copyright.[42]

Smith's statement was a lengthy reply to specific questions which Marshall had raised, and it asserted that his long experience in public office was proof that no conflict existed between his official duties and his religious convictions. The aspirant to the presidency then ended his open letter with the following testimony:

I summarize my creed as an American Catholic. I believe in worship of God according to the faith and practice of the Roman Catholic Church. I recognize no power in the institutions of my Church to interfere with the operations of the Constitution of the United States or the enforcement of the law of the land. I believe in the absolute freedom of conscience for all men and in equality of all churches, all sects, and all beliefs before the law as a matter of right and not as a matter of favor. I believe in the absolute separation of Church and State and in the strict enforcement of the provisions of the Constitution that Congress shall make no law respecting an establishment of religion or prohibiting the free exercise thereof. I believe that no tribunal of any church has any power to make any decree of force in the law of the land, other than to establish the status of its own communicants within its own church. I believe in the right of every parent to choose whether his child shall be educated in the public school or in a religious school supported by those of his own faith. I believe in the principle of noninterference by this country in the internal affairs of other nations and that we should stand steadfastly against such interference by whomsoever it may be urged. And I believe in the common brotherhood of man under the common fatherhood of God.

In this spirit I join with fellow Americans of all creeds in a fervent prayer that never again in this land will any public servant be challenged because of the faith in which he has tried to walk humbly with his God.[43]

This was the most explicit statement concerning personal religious outlook ever made by a presidential hopeful in the history of America up to that time. Being written, as it was, by a man who did not even want to make a statement in the first place, it was evidence of the intense concern with the religious issue which had pervaded American society. Smith hoped that his reply would settle the issue once and for all. This hope was echoed by a biographer of Smith, writing in 1927, who remarked that "The Marshall-Smith correspondence, published this year in the *Atlantic Monthly* and almost universally reprinted in the newspapers will prevent, it is probable, most of the open attacks on the Governor's religion."[44]

However, in 1927 almost anything which called attention to Roman Catholicism in America excited the imagination of those already fearful. Even this same biographer had to admit that some people would "continue to whisper threats of Papal domination."[45] Apparently nothing a prospective Catholic presidential candidate could say would have calmed the fears of some. Thus, instead of a cessation of the issue, the days following Smith's reply saw a new kind of attack. People now began saying that Smith had misrepresented Catholic doctrine. Some began to argue that if Smith were elected president the Catholic hierarchy would interfere even more in an effort to quell his independence.[46]

The New York governor refused to reply further, however. For him the issue had been settled. This was to be a bad mistake for Smith, for in fact, the issue had not been settled. Debates continued all around the country as people in the traditionally Protestant sections of the land began to realize more vividly that a Roman Catholic was moving closer and closer to the White House. The most vocal public figure at this stage was Senator Thomas J. Heflin of Alabama, who declared that there was a "Catholic Party" in the country and that Smith's aspirations for the presidency "represented the crowning effort of the Roman Catholic hierarchy to gain control of the White House."[47] Others adopted a calmer tone than Heflin but still maintained that there was danger in electing Smith.

In spite of all this the New York governor still remained the only real contender for the nomination. When he received it, the *New Republic* called it "a major miracle of American politics" in view of the staunch oppositon to Smith at the 1924 Democratic convention.[48] Though his nomination was an interesting political fact it was also a significant indication of some trends in American social and religious life. The very fact that Smith won the nomination of a major party demonstrates that by a decade after World War I Catholics in the country appeared strong enough to offset any disadvantage which anti-Catholicism might bring to a political party. Had this not been true no major party would have dared nominate a Roman Catholic in 1928. That the nomination of 1928 went to the same man whose nomination anti-Catholic forces had helped block just four years earlier shows how rapidly Catholicism was growing in American society. To nominate a Roman Catholic did not seem as much of a gamble in 1928.

But because—in spite of Senator Heflin's cries—there was no "Catholic Party" in the country and no guarantee that all Catholics would vote as a bloc, Smith's nomination was indication of newer Protestant attitudes as well. The very fact that he was nominated demonstrates some seeming improvement in Protestant-Catholic relations in the country by 1928. Anti-Catholicism seemed, at least to the Democratic party leaders, not to be as formidable as it had been earlier in the decade. There had been no major Klan riots for about four years and open conflict was not as much in evidence. At least some Protestants seemed to be adjusting to the presence of Roman Catholicism in America.

Nevertheless, improvement of a condition is by no means the same as its elimination, and by 1928 the nation still had not made a full adjustment to Catholicism. Al Smith's biggest mistake was that he failed to recognize the intensity of the fears that still remained. Smith's error, apparently, was an assumption that because the religious issue was settled in his mind it was settled in everyone else's mind as well. He made only passing reference to religion in his acceptance speech,[49] and as his campaign got started he named a Catholic, John J. Raskob, chairman of the Democratic National Committee. The appointment of Raskob hurt Smith, particularly in the South, and reinforced the fears of those who already thought that the Catholics were out to control the country,[50] but the Democratic candidate did not realize all this.

It was past mid-September before Smith realized that in spite of his hopes to the contrary his religious affiliation was definitely an issue. His daughter, who was accompanying him on a tour through the Central Plains, recalled later: "As we left Omaha and journeyed southward to Kansas and Oklahoma, ominous signs of bigotry appeared."[51] By the time they reached Oklahoma City Smith had decided to pull out all the stops. On six envelopes he made notes pertaining to religion. "Cry of Tammany is red herring," wrote Smith on one of the envelopes. "What lies behind [is] 'Religion.'"[52] When Smith faced his audience he began by denouncing Oklahoma's former senator, Robert L. Owen, who had bolted the Smith ticket on grounds of the New York governor's Tammany Hall connections, and then asserted that Owen was hiding the real reason. In strong language Smith declared that "at least once in this campaign I . . . owe it to the people of this country to discuss frankly and openly with them this attempt of Senator Owen and the forces behind him to inject bigotry, hatred, intolerance and un-American sectarian division into a campaign which should be an intelligent debate of the important issues which confront the American people." Smith maintained that he wanted no one to vote for him "on any religious grounds," but he further maintained that "any person who votes against me simply because of my religion is not, to my way of thinking, a good citizen."[53]

There was no doubt that Smith's Oklahoma City speech brought the religious issue into the open. After this the Democratic candidate made more frequent references to the religious issue, though none were so lengthy or so pointed as on the night of September 20 in Oklahoma City.[54] He still seemed to harbor the hope that the question would somehow go away.

The question would not go away, though. To some anti-Catholic forces Smith remained a "rum-soaked Romanist." To some people Smith simply embodied too many unfamiliar characteristics—his accent, his Tammany connections, his anti-prohibition stand, and his Roman Catholicism. The question of the repeal of prohibition was often linked with Smith's Catholicism, especially in the minds of Baptists and Methodists, many of whom were adamant toward any group which was "soft" on the issue of prohibition. Because so many Catholics seemingly supported repeal, the anti-Catholic sentiment among Baptists and Methodists grew even stronger, and sometimes those who opposed Smith on religious grounds *per se* used his stand on prohibition as a rationalization for their opposition.[55] In political circles some opponents of the Democratic nominee made frontal assaults on Smith's religion and his anti-prohibition stand. An example was Mrs. Willie Caldwell, a Republican committeewoman from Virginia, who declared in a circular letter that Herbert Hoover was depending on the women of America "in this hour of very vital moral religious crisis" to "save the United States from being Romanized and rum-ridden."[56] Hoover, who forthrightly condemned the entire whispering campaign against Smith, quickly repudiated Mrs. Caldwell's letter.[57]

In retrospect perhaps one of the most significant facts about the campaign was the relative silence of mainstream Protestantism over the religious issue. There were Protestant denunciations of the issue, such as the *Christian Century*'s labeling of the whispering campaign as "nonsensical and outrageous,"[58] but for the greater part, the Protestant mainstream did not put forth a concerted effort to counter the overt anti-Catholic forces in the country. In part this was due to the unfamiliarity of religion in general as a political question; responsible religious leaders were caught off guard and were unsure how to react. In part it was due, however, to the still remaining uneasiness in the minds of Protestant leaders over growing Catholic strength in America. Some Protestants were ready to stand back from an open anti-Catholicism, but not many were yet ready to stand openly against it. Fear of splitting Protestant ranks further—they were already split in the fundamentalist-modernist controversy—and thus having a weakened, divided Protestantism in America in face of a unified and growing Catholicism kept them from speaking out strongly against openly anti-Catholic forces.

After Smith lost the election by over six million popular votes a number of analyses were given. As could be expected, analysts drew various conclusions. Just how much Smith's Catholicism figured in the actual voting is still uncertain, but that it figured heavily is quite evident. As early as October 1 of that year a report from Kansas City, Missouri, stated that Smith's religion was the real issue in the minds of the people there.[59] Similar reports came later from other areas. In normally Democratic states that went for Hoover, like Tennessee, post-election analyses concluded that voters had gone to the polls "to vote against a Catholic."[60] Smith himself, who at one time had minimized the strength of anti-Catholic sentiment in the country, seemed convinced after the election that religion, not Tammany or prohibition or any other issue, was the most decisive factor in his defeat. In the words of one biographer, the Democratic nominee concluded that "while he might not have won in any circumstance, he had no chance to win because he was a Catholic."[61] In 1928 there were still too many Americans in whose minds an unwritten law barred a Catholic from the White House and to whom Roman Catholicism still appeared as a force alien to the American way of life.

Ill feelings and uneasiness are just part of the story of Protestant adjustment to Catholic growth, however. As in almost every context of conflict, there were those who were concerned for the improvement of attitudes, and there were occasions for an expression of this concern. Even though they made little headway in improving interfaith relations on a national scale at the time, the interfaith contacts of some of the servicemen in World War I were important seeds, later to grow into more positive emphases of brotherhood and good will. Everett Clinchy, a Protestant minister who later became director of the

National Conference of Christians and Jews (NCCJ), testified
that it was while serving in the army in 1917–1918 that he "came
to know and appreciate" Roman Catholics and Jews. "The interesting differences intrigued and enriched my thinking,"
states Clinchy.[62] His experiences, added to those of many others,
Catholic and Protestant alike, were to become a foundation for
a turn in a more positive direction which took place about a
decade after the war.

   Through the 1920s, positive interfaith efforts tended to focus
either on special days or special circumstances and for the most
part involved Jews as well as Protestants and Catholics. On
Christmas Eve 1920 a group called the American Committee
of the Rights of Religious Minorities, primarily Protestant but
with Catholic and some Jewish members as well, called on all
Americans "of good will to condemn every effort to arouse
divisive passions against any of our fellow countrymen" and "to
create a just and humane public sentiment that shall recognize
the Fatherhood of God and the brotherhood of man."[63] This
was the first tri-faith statement of opposition to religious and
racial prejudice in American history. Four years later when the
Federal Council of Churches held its annual convention in
Atlanta, a hotbed for Ku Klux Klan activity, there was enough
distress on the part of council leaders over why anyone reared
in Protestant Sunday schools would become a Klansman to
appoint a commission to study what Clinchy called the question "How does a Klansman get that way?"[64] The significance
of this commission lay not so much in its being a countermove
to the Klan but in its breaking ground for something more
permanent. Led by its secretary, the Reverend John Herring,
a Congregational minister, the commission brought together a
number of Protestants, Catholics, and Jews in an advisory
capacity and experimented with dinner meetings in several
cities.[65] Participants in various conferences during the 1920s
were Protestant clerical and lay leaders such as the Reverend S.
Parkes Cadman, president of the Federal Council of Churches,
Newton D. Baker, former secretary of war under Woodrow
Wilson, and Justice Charles Evans Hughes of the Supreme

Court, and Catholic leaders such as Monsignor Michael J. Lavelle of the archdiocese of New York, and Michael Williams, editor of *Commonweal*, Catholic lay periodical which began publication in 1924.[66]

It was in the year 1928 itself that these various efforts at interfaith cooperation began to solidify. Unquestionably, the major impetus was the emergence of the religious issue in the presidential campaign. Sterling Brown, president of the National Conference of Christians and Jews, cites the campaign as a central factor in the organization of the conference.[67] Catholic leaders were caught off guard by the issue and responsible Protestant leaders, particularly in the Federal Council, seemed to be embarrassed by the issue and by the council's failure to denounce openly the raising of the question of Governor Smith's religion. It was partly to avoid such an embarrassing predicament in the future that a solid push was made for a permanent nationwide interfaith organization.

It does not seem likely, though, that the campaign in and of itself was enough to bring about a permanent organization. In part, the time was simply ripe for this kind of venture. By election day 1928, one full decade to the month had passed since the end of World War I, and in that time America had gone from overt hostilities in Protestant-Catholic relations, epitomized by the Ku Klux Klan, through a climate of public debate in the mid-1920s, to the entry of religion in the national political arena. Now Americans were growing somewhat weary of the turmoil and, even though far from adjusted to religious pluralism, were ready to welcome a more affirmative approach. Though the 1928 campaign helped to bring on the weariness, no doubt it would have soon come about even without the campaign, for the nation simply could not sustain its religious conflicts at the fever pitch where they had been for so much of the decade.

Aware that the time was ripe for something permanent and hoping to head off the possibility of a new rise of interfaith conflicts in the future, several of the men involved in interfaith discussions which were going on formed a "Conference of Jews

and Christians," with Charles Evans Hughes writing a circular
letter of endorsement for the organization. In the fall of 1928,
the group along with the Federal Council of Churches' Committee on Goodwill Between Christians and Jews invited Everett Clinchy to direct a national organization, and from this
the permanent organization of the National Conference of
Jews and Christians, later to be known as National Conference
of Christians and Jews, emerged.[68]

There was a bit more to the title of the organization than
some of its early participants recognized, for in saying "Christians" rather than "Protestants and Catholics" there was an
implied admission of some basic theological unity between
these two religious establishments. Including Judaism in American interfaith activities, therefore, was a boost to the improvement of Protestant-Catholic relations. It marked the first time
in American life that a non-Christian religion had been involved in a widescale organization with either Protestants or
Catholics, and the differences, real or imagined, which members
of each of the latter two groups sensed with Judaism probably
helped bring on a feeling of at least a bit of theological kinship
between them. Will Herberg, prominent American Jewish
sociologist in his book *Protestant-Catholic-Jew* refers to the
designation "Christians and Jews" as theological rather than
sociological.[69]

It would be a mistake, however, to assume that the organization was theological in substance. One of its early Catholic
participants testified that at no time could he recall "publicly
discussing religion" in any of the NCCJ programs.[70] Furthermore, even in face of its official title many of the publications
and official statements of the organization still referred to
"Protestants, Catholics and Jews," and numerous people called
it by the tripartite title.[71]

One of the principal reasons for a lack of theological focus
in the NCCJ lay in the fact that Americans simply were not
theologically oriented. It is a peculiar but real fact of American
life that people can get extremely upset about the presence of
another religious group without comprehending anything of

theological substance about either faith. This in part reflects America's lack of an intellectual emphasis, which has permeated its religious establishments as well as its other areas of public and private life. To have attempted anything in the way of theological dialogue during the first two to three decades after World War I would have simply been too complex an undertaking for most Americans.

To arouse the interest and support of Americans, early interfaith activities had to be social and political in emphasis. American people tended not so much to *have* religion in the sense of strong convictions as to *use* religion to further their own social and political desires. Hence, they easily sensed threats to their social and political positions on the part of other religious groups. All the basic religious conflicts in America leading up to the emergence of the NCCJ had been based on considerations other than dogma. The Klan's religious overtones came from ethnic fears. It had no ecclesiastical doctrine but rather desired a "one hundred percent Americanism," with which it felt the Catholic church's ties to Rome conflicted. Doctrinal reasons for the Catholic's loyalty to Papal authority were simply not of concern to the nativist. The nativist's concern was that the Catholic did have this loyalty, and this concern was political. Furthermore, had the interfaith conflicts been primarily doctrinal, Catholicism would never have become an issue in the 1928 campaign. And as the Protestants emphasized the social and political aspects of American Catholicism, Catholics in America increased their own emphasis upon themselves as a social and political phenomenon and left their considerations of dogma, insofar as the general public was concerned, in the background. A definite indication of this was an opening article in a Catholic-Protestant dialogue in the *Forum* magazine in 1925 when the author, Michael Williams, editor of *Commonweal*, titled his remarks "The Roman Catholic Church—An American Institution."[72] It was expedient, therefore, for any organization that wished to improve the climate of interfaith relationships in America to take on a political and social emphasis. Early participants in the NCCJ aided this image in that they included Charles Evans Hughes of the Supreme Court and Newton D. Baker, who had been secretary of war under Woodrow Wilson.

Finally, among those who did comprehend theological matters there was still a reticence to engage in discussions of doctrine and dogma. The first two decades after World War I were still pre-ecumenical days, especially in America. There was not yet enough mutual trust and understanding between Protestants and Catholics for either to want to lay fundamental assumptions on the line in front of the other. Everett Clinchy recalls that in the early days of the National Conference of Christians and Jews the organization had to assure "rigid Christian theologians," especially Catholics and conservative Protestants, that it would limit its scope of activities to civic contexts and at the most to "natural" or "rational" religion rather than to revealed religion.[73]

In the long run this lack of dialogue about basic theological concepts was to hurt the effectiveness of the NCCJ; Protestants and Catholics failed to achieve genuine understanding of one another at the deeper levels. But the characteristic that limited NCCJ's long-range success helped make it successful in its early days. Guaranteed safety from embarrassing discussions of dogma and given the excitement of a new kind of political and social endeavor, numerous people—Protestant, Catholic, and Jewish—began taking part in NCCJ programs.

The first major undertaking of the NCCJ was a seminar at Columbia University in January 1929. It was at the suggestion of Al Smith himself, on whom the new director Everett Clinchy had called in December 1928, that Columbia's President Nicholas Murray Butler, a Republican and a Protestant, gave the keynote address.[74] There on the walls of the room in which the opening session was held were displayed numerous pieces of anti-Catholic literature and several caricatures used against Al Smith in the campaign which still echoed through the country.[75]

Late in 1929, the entire cause of interfaith cooperation was given an unexpected boost—though from an unwelcome source—with the beginning of the Depression. The Depression affected the dynamics of interfaith relationships in much the same manner as had World War I. It forced people of both Protestant and Catholic orientations to submerge their differences in face of a common threat. During World War I it had been for the protection of national security; during the Depression it was for the sake of economic survival. Even in religious circles, stomachs seemed more important than souls during a time when there were breadlines and lean-to shanty towns. Threats of Papal domination from far-off Rome, where many had never been anyway, seemed remote in comparison to threats of permanent financial ruin, of which jobless people in one's own circle of associates and closed business enterprises in one's hometown were daily reminders. For Catholics, who despite their rapid numerical growth through the 1920s were still a definite minority, there was a recognizable dependence on non-Catholic sources for needed aid. In such circumstances Catholics were much more prone to watch their steps in order to keep from offending their Protestant fellow citizens who held a preponderance of economic power.

Thus, as in any crisis where common interests are threatened and common needs are involved, adversaries found themselves forced to work together. Cooperation by all Americans was absolutely essential during the Depression years. Hence, the elimination of religious bickerings and some type of expression of good will and common purpose between Protestants and Catholics throughout the country was not only deemed right but also quite desirable. For once in American history economics definitely affected interfaith attitudes.

One of the most definite examples of the effect of the Depression on Protestant-Catholic relationships was found in the radio broadcasts of Charles E. Coughlin, a Roman Catholic priest in the Detroit suburb of Royal Oak, Michigan. Describing himself as "a simple Catholic priest endeavoring to inject Christianity into the fabric of an economic system woven upon the loom of greed,"[76] Father Coughlin began shortly after the stock market crash to turn his series of radio sermons into commentaries on the economic plight of the nation. From 1930 till 1935 his central theme was that of the pitiful economic plight of the American people and how selfish interests of a privileged few threatened to make the plight even worse.[77]

During the early 1930s Father Coughlin became a figure around whom discontented masses of Americans could rally. He voiced the frustrations of many Americans, both Catholic and Protestant. Consequently, this priest of the Roman Catholic Church gained widespread support in Protestant-oriented areas that had formerly been openly antagonistic toward Catholicism. In the face of dire economic needs the clerical collar of the Roman church seemed much less threatening. *Commonweal* in 1931 reported large numbers of contributions from Protestants to Father Coughlin's broadcasts[78]—a noteworthy fact in view of the financial weakness of so many people by that time. Some Protestant editors gave Father Coughlin favorable comments. An example was Albert C. Dieffenbach, a Unitarian and religious editor of the *Boston Evening Transcript*, who praised the Catholic church for allowing Coughlin to speak so freely and agreed with the priest's statement that "it is the business of spiritual leaders to concern themselves with the material welfare of their followers."[79] Even more forceful was the *Michigan Christian Advocate*, a Methodist-Episcopal weekly, in stating that the Royal Oak priest "is breaking down the prejudice of the masses of Protestants against the Catholic Church. Thousands of Protestants hail Father Coughlin as their friend, their militant defender and their one courageous advocate, a prophet of the prophets."[80] The Protestant support of Father Coughlin was strong enough in the first five years of the 1930s for even the *Ladies Home Journal* to take notice and to suggest that the priest's " 'soak the rich' " themes had perhaps "broken down some of the barriers of religious prejudice."[81]

By the middle of the decade, Father Coughlin turned more directly to politics. In 1935 he broke with President Roosevelt's New Deal policies, and the following year his National Union for Social Justice put forth presidential and vice-presidential candidates. In terms of the submergence of religious concerns by economic concerns, it is noteworthy that the presidential candidate, Congressman William Lemke of North Dakota, was Protestant and his running mate, Thomas Charles O'Brien, former district attorney of Boston, was Catholic.[82] By this time, however, Coughlin's support from many sources was waning and he was no longer the rallying point for the economically disenchanted to the extent that he had been earlier. After 1936, when he became an isolationist and definitely anti-Semitic, he enjoyed even less support, Catholic as well as non-Catholic.[83] In the earlier 1930s, however, while the Depression was at its depth, his public support demonstrated that Protestants and Catholics could—at least temporarily—overlook their conflicts in order to fight for common economic needs.

Further demonstration of the effect of the economic distress of the Depression on the improvement of interfaith relations is seen in some of the express concerns of the NCCJ. In March 1933 soon after Franklin Delano Roosevelt had taken office as president, the NCCJ sponsored a manifesto calling for federal government action to relieve unemployment, improve labor relations, effect tax reforms, and guarantee old age benefits. Signing the manifesto were 160 well-known clergymen and laymen from all three major faiths in America.[84] This support by influential religious leaders continued generally unshaken as the New Deal became a reality. In 1935 at the first session of an NCCJ-sponsored biannual Institute on Human Relations held in Williamstown, Massachusetts, Protestants and Catholics from across the nation joined with Jewish participants in support of the basic New Deal philosophy. A correspondent to *Nation* magazine wrote of the speech Frank Porter Graham, president of University of North Carolina, made there on behalf of government social controls: "If Mr. Roosevelt is wise he will make this [speech] exhibit number one in behalf of the New Deal in the campaign a year hence."[85] This Williamstown interfaith meeting held sessions on history, economics, sociology, and other areas in an effort "to apply the social sciences to inter-group relations." Specific New Deal measures, such as social security, and their relevance to relationships among the groups were discussed also.[86] All this was further demonstration

of how the Depression was drawing people of the various religious traditions in America together. Even as late as 1939 the
Williamstown Institute concerned itself, among other things,
with the church's role in economic reform and social welfare.[87]

By providing a specific program that both Protestant and
Catholic leaders in America could support, the New Deal became a catalyst for interfaith activities in the 1930s. Having
discovered one common affirmation, that of the necessity of
government intervention in the nation's economy, it was a bit
easier for religious leaders to seek other areas of agreement in
the social and economic spheres. The New Deal, therefore, in
reality influenced the cause of interfaith cooperation more
extensively by its indirect encouragement of this cooperation
than the direct religious support of the New Deal influenced
the government's economic programs.

It would be inaccurate, however, to think that the economy
was the sole sphere of interfaith concerns during the 1930s. Interfaith activities, especially those of the NCCJ, included a
variety of projects. A genuine concern for the elimination of
religious prejudices was manifest in an emphasis on national
brotherhood. Everett Clinchy relates that the idea emerged in
a conversation he had in Denver with a Roman Catholic priest
named Father McMerramin. Not wanting to leave brotherhood
in the field of idle talk, the NCCJ director set in motion plans
leading to Brotherhood Week, which essentially centered in
one national day of brotherhood.[88] Brotherhood Day was first
observed on April 29, 1934, with S. Parkes Cadman of the Federal Council of Churches (also an NCCJ chairman) declaring
in his announcement of the observance that "Hatred and Suspicion of those of other faiths are foreign to the spirit of religion."[89] The NCCJ had set aside Brotherhood Day, said
Cadman, "to emphasize the moral obligations of the essential
teachings of the three great religious groups in America."[90]
Two years later President Roosevelt endorsed the observance,
and in 1938 he became the honorary chairman of a committee
designed to incorporate Brotherhood Day into a celebration of
the tenth anniversary of the NCCJ.[91] That year, a Brotherhood

Day pledge titled "Ten Commandments of Good Will" was recited in some two thousand American communities. It read:

> I will honor all men and women regardless of their race or religion.
>
> I will protect and defend my neighbor and my neighbor's children
> against the ravages of racial or religious bigotry.
>
> I will exemplify in my own life the spirit of good will and
> understanding.
>
> I will challenge the philosophy of racial superiority by whomsoever
> that philosophy may be proclaimed, be these persons kings, emperors,
> dictators or demagogues.
>
> I will refuse to join or be identified with any organization that has
> for its purpose the spreading of anti-Semitism, anti-Catholicism, or
> anti-Protestantism.
>
> I will protest against every manifestation of racial or religious
> prejudice.
>
> I will do more than live and let live; I will live and help live.
>
> I will, until my dying day, establish comradeship with all those who
> seek to exalt the spirit of love and reconciliation throughout the
> world.
>
> I will not be misled by the lying propaganda of those who seek to
> set race against race or nation against nation.
>
> I will be all things to all men; to the Jew I will be a Jew, to the
> Christian a Christian, nor will I be divorced from this purpose by
> threats of personal violence or of social ostracism, so help me God.[92]

The elevated language of the pledge undoubtedly produced
high emotions on the part of some who recited it. There are
no figures, however, to indicate just how much eradication of
interfaith tensions occurred because of the pledge. At root
there seems to have been very little, for just a year later
Protestant-Catholic conflicts erupted into the open again with
the appointment by Roosevelt of Myron Taylor as a representative to the Vatican. As is the case in many pledges, the
"Ten Commandments of Good Will" no doubt led some to the
mistaken idea that because they had recited a pledge they had
fulfilled its ideals. Unwittingly, therefore, the pledge could
have caused some people to let their guard down and to become
even more vulnerable to interfaith tensions. Nevertheless, the
pledge was a noble venture, the first of its kind in twentieth-
century America, and doubtless did confirm the desires for

brotherhood and good will felt by numerous people of all three faiths.

The pledge also shows how closely the concern for eradication of religious bigotry was tied to other concerns. This typifies a feeling long existent in America that religious concerns, given the context of the entire population, do not exist in themselves—this in face of the precept of separation of church and state. Improved Protestant-Catholic relations, therefore, were desirable primarily because they were good for the nation and only secondarily because they were consistent with the basic tenets of each religious body. This underscores a general assumption in the nation that separation of church and state exists more for the good of the state than for the good of the church. It is the state which is to be protected by this concept.

The Brotherhood Day pledge and the various other good-will projects of the 1930s, however, though endorsed by the state through some of its officials, were not originated by the state. It remained the genius of the country's religious leadership, through groups like the NCCJ and the Federal Council, to initiate and bring about the good-will efforts. Final credit, therefore, must belong to the religious rather than the political establishments.

Among the other interfaith projects of this decade of emphasis on good will and brotherhood were NCCJ-sponsored local "round tables," permanent committees of citizens from various religious and racial groups in the community, who would sponsor discussions involving Protestant, Catholic, and Jewish participants. By 1938 there were 1,150 of these.[93] There were also several nationwide tours sponsored by the NCCJ and featuring a Protestant clergyman, a Roman Catholic priest, and a Jewish rabbi traveling together to promote the good-will and brotherhood themes.[94] Youth of the country received their share of attention from interfaith workers and the tangible evidence of this included publications such as a booklet called *New Relationships with Jews and Catholics* "to meet the increasing demand of Protestant young people who are interested in resolving misunderstandings arising from religious differences in interfaith groups."[95] Then there were the area and national seminars. Most noted of these was the biannual Williamstown Institute of Human Relations, begun in 1935 as a successor to the Williamstown Institute of Politics. The purpose of this project was to bring Protestant, Catholic, and Jewish leaders together for intensified discussions of common concerns and goals. Both *Commonweal* and the *Christian Century* endorsed the project, the latter praising it as "the first undertaking of this kind on this continent."[96] The widespread interest in the amelioration of interfaith antipathies was demonstrated in the attendance at the initial session of 1935. Plans had been made for 100 participants; 685 attended, including 375 Protestants and 135 Roman Catholics.[97] Discussion centered chiefly on the matters of religious persecutions in nations such as Mexico and Germany and on lessons America might learn from it all. Also, in an action demonstrating the Depression's influence on interfaith cooperation, the institute endorsed the New Deal efforts by the government.[98]

When the 1935 session ended, the *Christian Century* reported that five areas of general agreement had been reached: the primacy of the spiritual, the necessity of unity in the struggle for social justice, the goals of social justice (which were not defined by the periodical), the peril of totalitarian forms of nationalism, and the understanding of religious and racial prejudice as an adult problem.[99] The next edition of the *Christian Century*, however, exposed the major weakness of the entire brotherhood movement of the 1930s by observing that even though the participants in the Williamstown Institute could discuss and debate they could not worship together. The Protestant publication pointed out that Roman Catholic tradition would have prevented it.[100] Undoubtedly the emotions of many of the Protestant participants would also have prevented it. The magazine added the prophetic note that "Until men are able to worship together, the religious contribution to the problems of human relations must be distinctly limited."

It was this lack of an explicitly religious dimension that was to cause the good-will emphasis to wane in the face of new conflicts that arose in 1939 and 1940. In spite of all their social and political implications, ultimately the relations of Catholics and Protestants are a religious problem, for they involve religious identities and religious traditions older than America itself. To ignore the explicitly doctrinal and theological matters, therefore, is to ignore the deepest levels of interfaith relationships and to give emphasis to the improvement of attitudes that have comparatively shallow roots. The approach adopted by the good-will movement actually was a negative rather than an affirmative one, on two counts. It became an emphasis on the *avoidance* of conflict, and it assumed that in order to avoid conflict one had to avoid theological exchange.

Because the interfaith efforts did avoid theological exchange Protestant and Catholic scholars and theologians in America during the 1920s and 1930s continued to write about each other's traditions with little real comprehension. And since people generally are prone to judge the position of others in terms of their own presuppositions, the doctrinal writings during the period of emphasis on external good will and brotherhood continued to be quite polemic. For example, Carlton J. H. Hayes, a prominent historian and Catholic co-chairman of the National Conference of Christians and Jews, wrote in 1932 in the *Catholic Historical Review* that "an excess of religious intolerance" was directly and primarily related to the "religious upheaval of the sixteenth century." He blamed the Reformation for diminishing the power and influence of Christianity in the modern world. Though Hayes wrote as an historian, it was rather evident that he wrote primarily as a man who was a thoroughgoing Roman Catholic with strong feelings of estrangement from the Protestant movement, feelings that his participation in the brotherhood movement had not lessened.[101]

An even more striking example of the lack of appreciation for Protestant emphases came from the pen of the Reverend John A. O'Brien of Notre Dame, who was also an active participant in the good-will program of the 1930s. In 1938, the same year that the Brotherhood Day pledge "Ten Commandments of Good Will" was released, O'Brien wrote in a treatise on the merits of Catholicism that "religious indifferentism" was "the twentieth century harvest of the seeds of religious chaos and anarchy which were sown by the misguided reformers in the sixteenth century." [102]

American Protestants likewise betrayed a lack of appreciation for Roman Catholic thought during the 1920s and 1930s. This lack of appreciation is seen best in the noticeable absence of writings on Catholicism by reputable Protestant scholars in America. Writings that did appear tended to lay heavy stress on Protestant corrections of Catholic errors. An example was John T. McNeill of the University of Chicago, who wrote in the *Journal of Religion* in 1928 that it was Rome, not the reformers, that disrupted the unity of the universal church by its apostasy of Christian doctrine.[103] In a similar vein David S. Schaff of Union Theological Seminary in New York wrote in the *Union Seminary Review* (of Union Seminary in Richmond, Virginia) in 1931 that the Protestant reformers had "invented no new truth any more than Columbus and the Cabots created a new world in the West." What they did, said Schaff, was merely to return to "truths which had been forgotten or buried beneath the traditions of men." [104]

Examples such as these indicate that even among the better informed Catholic and Protestant leaders their differences still preyed more upon their minds than did any possible basis for unity. Ecclesiastical unity was, in fact, hardly a topic for consideration during the 1920s and 1930s. The Papal encyclical *Lux Veritatus* of 1931 calling for the unification of all Christendom under the banner of Rome was denounced with vehemence by Protestant spokesmen in America, including one Methodist bishop from North Carolina who invited the Pope to become a Methodist! [105] An effort at Christmas 1935 by a group of high-church Episcopal clergymen and laymen in America to promote a reunion with Roman Catholicism resulted, rather, in Protestant leaders' attacking Roman Catholic theology in a strong demonstration of opposition to any such idea.[106]

The lack of theological and ecclesiastical depth in the good-will and brotherhood movement does not, however, diminish the importance of these emphases. In actuality, the ultimate weakness of the movement was its immediate strength. Leaders of NCCJ and other interfaith groups realized that religion in America was still in a definitely pre-ecumenical stage, and they geared their programs accordingly. By keeping things on a nondoctrinal basis they were able to bring more people into their ranks than they could have otherwise. As Everett Clinchy put it, "Assured that NCCJ would limit its range to the civic areas, to 'natural' or rational religion, even rigid Christian theologians would meet with people outside their faith." "Clearly NCCJ had to start this way," said Clinchy.[107]

The emphases upon brotherhood and good will were, in fact, quite successful in keeping down open conflict between Catholics and Protestants throughout the entire decade of the 1930s. During that decade there were no large-scale anti-Catholic or anti-Protestant demonstrations such as had occurred during the 1920s. The Ku Klux Klan was in decline, and as evidence of the strong sentiment in America for interfaith good will, the Klan purposely avoided strong anti-Catholic and anti-Semitic, as well as anti-Negro, efforts during the 1930s. When Justice Hugo Black, Roosevelt's appointee to the Supreme Court in 1937, was seen to have had Klan connections during the 1920s, both Catholic and Protestant leaders in America expressed deep concern. Such potential trouble areas as Black's connections or Father Coughlin's diatribes never gave rise to serious nationwide interfaith controversies. The sentiment for cordial relationships was simply too strong. In final analysis, the National Conference of Christians and Jews more than the Depression deserves the credit for bringing about this desire for better interfaith attitudes. As mentioned earlier, the economic crisis of the 1930s did much to submerge the mutual Protestant-Catholic hostilities of the 1920s as both groups found their domestic energies turned toward economic survival. However, one must bear in mind that the National Conference of Christians and Jews came into being a year before the stock market crash, and that even prior to 1928 some leaders in the NCCJ and in interfaith activities in general had already been laying groundwork. And since the content of interfaith activities in the 1930s went a good bit beyond the discussion of economic matters it is evident that the brotherhood movement was concerned with more than economic expediency. Its participants genuinely wanted better relations. Had the attainment of better relations between Catholics and Protestants been left entirely up to nonecclesiastical sources, nothing of the magnitude of a nationwide emphasis on brotherhood and good will, lasting in intensity for more than a decade, would have occurred. Matters affecting the attitudes of religious bodies must ultimately have the cooperation of the members of those bodies. This cooperation came about through a realization on the part of thoughtful leaders of both faiths that animosity hurts the group feeling it as much if not more than the group toward which it is directed. The brotherhood emphasis, therefore, was in the eyes of its proponents a matter of religious survival as much as it was of economic survival. In essence the emphasis was a reaction to the interfaith antagonisms of the 1920s. And both the conflicts of the 1920s and the good-will efforts of the 1930s were the results of American Protestantism's trying to adjust to Catholic growth and of Catholicism's trying to secure a permanent influence in the country.

II.

Catholicism in America Comes of Age: 1939-1955

Early in 1939 Everett Clinchy of the National Conference of Christians and Jews spoke of an "unparalleled spirit of cooperation" existing among religious groups in America.[1] One month later the calm interfaith waters rippled with a new wave of conflict. In that month, February, Pope Pius XI died, and when the new Pope, Pius XII, was crowned, among those present was Joseph P. Kennedy, United States ambassador to Great Britain and a Roman Catholic—as the official representative of President Franklin D. Roosevelt.

Roosevelt's action in sending Kennedy to the Papal coronation was an extremely significant step. Not only was it the first time that a president of the United States had had a personal representative at an ecclesiastical ceremony of such magnitude, it was also a recognition by the president of a new status for Catholicism in America. Until this time American political leaders had generally acted toward Rome as being principally the headquarters of a growing but minority religious body in the country. But with the sending of Kennedy in an official capacity to the coronation the president was acknowledging that these headquarters were of worldwide importance. By doing this the president bestowed new dignity and significance upon the Catholic church in America.

Protestants were quick to sense this, much quicker than was the president himself. For Roosevelt, Kennedy's presence at the coronation amounted to a simple acknowledgment of the political importance of the Papacy. But for numerous Protestant churchmen it was tantamount to giving the Roman Catholic Church preferential treatment. Shortly after the appointment the executive board of the United Lutheran Church in America and the annual meeting of the Southern Baptist Convention both publicly denounced Roosevelt's move. The latter called it a "dangerous tendency toward the union of church and state."[2]

Had Roosevelt's actions stopped with Kennedy's presence at the crowning of Pius XII the furor might have subsided. A coronation is, after all, a single and short-lived event, and the themes of good will and brotherhood were still ringing in the ears of many Americans. But late in 1939 the president announced the appointment of Myron C. Taylor, former head of United States Steel, as ambassador without portfolio to the Vatican. In his capacity as chief of state, Roosevelt looked upon the appointment of Taylor as strictly a political move, one to promote world peace.

However, the appointment gave the entire matter of White House-Vatican connections a look of permanency. This in itself was enough to upset those who felt that any official relations between political and ecclesiastical sources was in violation of the principle of the separation of church and state. It made no difference to those who felt this way that Taylor was himself an Episcopalian. The principle stood whether the appointee was a Catholic, an Episcopalian, a Baptist, or an atheist. There should be no official church-state interaction of any kind.

Furthermore, by implication the appointment of Taylor to the Vatican was further acknowledgment by official political circles of the importance of the Roman Catholic Church in world, and hence in American, affairs. This did more than any simple numerical growth to instill in American Catholics a new sense of pride.[3] From this point on for over a decade the Catholic church in America became more and more openly aggressive in demanding recognition in all phases of American life.

For Protestants the appointment was a sudden reminder that Roman Catholicism in America was indeed growing both in numbers and influence. This fact had not been much emphasized during the years just prior to Taylor's appointment, but once the appointment brought Catholic growth again to public attention, the submerged suspicions of American Protestants toward American Catholics rose to the surface. Protestants from many backgrounds felt that the Roman Catholic Church sought political advantage in American life and that the Catholic hierarchy would do anything necessary to secure that advantage. In turn, the feeling of Catholics that Protestants were trying to keep them from having equal opportunities for growth in America was renewed. In truth, each group began to see more enemies in the other's camp than really existed. Every public notice of a Catholic figure was deemed by some Protestants an effort on the part of Rome to gain control of the power structure of the United States, and every expression of belief in absolute church-state separation by Protestants was seen by some Catholics as an attempt to weaken Catholicism and to hold it back.

The overt demonstrations of these attitudes were evidence that the mutual suspicions that had existed after World War I had not really been weakened by the brotherhood emphasis of the 1930s. The suspicions and basic conflicts must still have been strong to have burst into the open so quickly and so forcefully with the singular action of FDR's appointment of Myron Taylor to the Vatican. The Vatican representative issue did not create Protestant-Catholic tensions; it simply called them forth once again.

Roosevelt himself seems to have sensed the presence of religious tensions, for concurrently with the announcement of Taylor's appointment the chief executive called George Buttrick, president of the Federal Council of Churches, and Cyrus Adler, president of the Jewish Theological Seminary, to the White House.[4] A few days later Roosevelt met with Baptist, Lutheran, and Seventh Day Adventist leaders.[5] An air of secrecy surrounded both of these meetings and no one involved would make any specific statement as to what was said. A statement later that month from the Executive Committee of the Federal Council of Churches indicated opposition to the Taylor mission if it should "unfortunately prove a stepping stone to a permanent diplomatic relationship" but implied cautious support on the assumption that the appointment was "strictly temporary, unofficial, and centrally concerned with efforts for world peace."[6] This is possibly an indication that Roosevelt, in his conversations with Buttrick and others, was himself not clear as to the future of the mission.

It is fairly certain, though, that Roosevelt, by meeting with Protestant and Jewish leaders, hoped to prevent a public outcry over the appointment. Undoubtedly he still remembered with some anxiety the opposition to his sending Ambassador Kennedy to the Papal coronation. But his hopes were in vain. By May 1940 over twenty-five Protestant groups, representing a cross-section of American Protestantism, had either protested the Taylor mission or had requested Taylor's recall.[7]

There seem to have been at least three strands of Protestant opposition to the Taylor mission. There were those who opposed it out of genuine disapproval of any kind of public acknowledgment by the government of any religious group whatsoever. There were others who opposed it largely because there was no Protestant parallel to it: a speaker on the nationwide radio program "The Lutheran Hour" called the appointment of Taylor "an unmistakable preference for one church group."[8] Then there were those who opposed the Taylor post primarily because its context was the Catholic church. This was the most subtle of attitudes, for many who held it were not aware that their feeling was not so much one of opposition to a presidential representative to a religious leader as it was a fear of Catholic growth in the country. Some Protestants seemed almost to have repented for having let their guard down during the brotherhood era, feeling that Rome had taken advantage of the emphasis on good will to secure a political advantage in America.

These attitudes, of course, were often mingled together in the same people. But even where they were not mingled, the opposition to the whole idea of a representative at the Vatican was so intense that there was no significant in-fighting among Protestants as to the form the opposition should take. This unity of opposition to the Taylor mission led some Catholics to see all of Protestantism as one antagonistic anti-Catholic force and sometimes to mistake genuine concern on the part of some Protestants for bigotry. Catholics also pressed the cause of Taylor's mission further. In May 1940 the Most Reverend James H. Ryan, Bishop of Omaha, called for full diplomatic relations with the Vatican.[9]

From this point on the brotherhood movement in the country was powerless to stem the rising tide of conflict. When Everett Clinchy of the National Conference of Christians and Jews made his annual report in 1940 he noted that the Taylor mission had given rise to "an ominous situation . . . with regard to Roman Catholic and Protestant relations."[10] The "ominous situation" was in reality the beginning of a new era in Protestant-Catholic relations in America, an era of mutual misunderstandings, severe stress, and widespread charges and countercharges. By the end of 1940 the brotherhood emphasis was all but forgotten on a nationwide scale, although the National Conference of Christians and Jews continued valiantly to stress this ideal. In place of good will there was a revival of the open conflicts of the 1920s.

There were some noticeable differences between the 1920s and the new era of open conflicts, however. In the 1920s, although Protestant reaction to Roman Catholic growth was certainly nationwide, the overt demonstrations against Catholicism came largely from reactionary segments of the non-Catholic population and were generally led by people with little or no ecclesiastical training. In the 1940s and early 1950s the open reaction against Catholicism came from all kinds of American Protestants, moderate and liberal as well as conservative, and was often led by well-trained clergymen and well-educated laymen. This difference accounts largely for the difference in form between the conflicts of the 1920s and those of the 1940s. Under the banner of quickly formed reactionary groups and men of little training the anti-Catholicism of the 1920s had taken the form of crusades and sometimes violence. Under the leadership of more firmly established bodies and more highly educated men, the anti-Catholicism of the 1940s was expressed in the more sophisticated forms of resolutions, manifestos, and political activism. Furthermore, the elements of leadership found in the conflicts of the 1940s and early 1950s gave the entire reaction to Roman Catholicism in America a more definite ecclesiastical base and a new aura of respectability. The anti-Catholic activities of the 1920s had not been publicly endorsed by major Protestant communities in the nation. In the 1940s and early 1950s such activities often enjoyed the sponsorship of prominent Protestant groups.

Another striking element in the new era of conflict was the attitude of American Catholicism itself. Throughout the 1920s the Catholic community in America seemed somewhat shy in the face of Protestant reaction. Although in self-defense Catholics had begun new periodicals and had denounced groups like the Ku Klux Klan, the entire Catholic establishment in America had not presented an organized front. The pattern for Catholics had been one of retreating into the security of numbers, by grouping themselves into entirely Catholic neighborhoods and maintaining their own schools without making a national issue of it. Catholic voices had been raised sporadically rather than continuously during the 1920s. The pattern changed, however, in the 1940s. There was a new aggressiveness on the part of American Catholics. One of the first signs of this was the public support by the Catholic hierarchy of an all-Catholic slate in the Cleveland, Ohio, public school board elections in 1940.[11] Though three of the four members of the slate were defeated,[12] the Cleveland incident indicated a growing feeling of self-confidence on the part of Catholics generally. Catholics were now ready to use more open and forceful efforts to gain their goals.

One reason for this new aggressiveness was that the Catholic church in America now had a greater security of numbers. Though still a numerical minority, it no longer had a minority consciousness. By 1940 American Catholics numbered 21,403,000, an increase of 1,199,000 during the previous decade and of 3,667,000 since 1920.[13] By 1944 Catholics numbered first among church members in thirty-eight of America's fifty largest cities and were more numerous than any one Protestant denomination in the country.[14] Roman Catholic descendants of the new immigration no longer held an immigrant consciousness. By 1940 they were second- and third-generation Americans. They were extensively familiar with the American political structures and were more confident than ever before about working through them. It was en era in which Catholicism was coming of age in America and thereby was asserting itself more freely and more openly.

The lines were drawn, therefore, for renewed interfaith struggles. Protestants, accustomed to having the major influence in American religious life, and Catholics, feeling a new confidence in their own strength and becoming increasingly aggressive, made the struggle almost inevitable. In a sense, the conflict resembled a generation battle between older, more established adults and youth reaching adulthood, the former recalling long years of effort at establishing their influence and not wanting their efforts uprooted, the latter realizing a new potential for influence and impatient to be seen and heard.

The intensity of the conflict is suggested in part by the fact that not even during World War II was there an explicit national emphasis on interfaith good will comparable to the brotherhood movement of the previous decade. Even though war effort lessened some of the public furor between Catholics and Protestants, the tensions remained. The *Christian Century* confessed in 1943 that "American Protestantism is striving to reorient its forces" and gave as a major "source of pressure" the "growing power of Roman Catholicism in the political and social life of the nation."[15]

Protestant recognition of new Catholic power was strikingly articulated in a series of articles by Harold Fey, published in the *Christian Century* in 1944–1945 under the collective title "Can Catholicism Win America?" Especially significant were these remarks in the introductory article:

Today the influence of the Roman Catholic Church is greater than it has ever been in this country, and it is increasing steadily. The last federal census of religious bodies showed that this body stood first in the number of church members in thirty eight of our fifty largest cities. When it is remembered that it is the cities which set the pace in our culture, the importance of this predominance becomes apparent. While Catholics are not so numerous as the membership of all Protestant bodies combined, they are more numerous than the membership of any single Protestant denomination in the nation at large and in thirty five of the forty eight states. Their 22,945,247 communicants constitute a denomination almost three times as large as the Methodist Church, the largest Protestant denomination. The ideas and intentions by which this great body is dominated are therefore of great importance in determining the direction in which our national life is going to develop. This is a matter of special concern because, unlike members of nearly all other churches, these millions of American citizens are subject to the spiritual direction of an Italian pontiff who represents a culture historically alien to American institutions.

An appraisal is particularly timely just now because the Roman Catholic hierarchy has changed its fundamental strategy in this country in the past generation. The results of this change are becoming apparent.

The leaders of the Catholic Church in America have for the first time begun to plan and function *as a unit* on questions which affect the status of the church in our national life. In this period they have developed an organizational structure which enables them to do this systematically, thoroughly, and without intermission. They have cast off the inferiority complex which naturally characterizes an alien minority and have begun boldly and aggressively to assert their power.

It is only within this generation that the Roman Catholic Church has come to feel at home in the United States. Now that it speaks the "American" language and has raised up native leaders who are loyally followed by millions, it is for the first time in a position to make history—American history.[16]

These observations and comments articulated what scores of American Protestants had sensed. Catholicism was moving in America with a new confidence which many Protestants feared could make Catholicism's influence predominant throughout the society. In the series of articles that followed, Fey stressed that Roman Catholics were making considerable progress among certain groups that had previously been predominantly Protestant, especially Negroes, workers, and farmers. From this he concluded that "The Roman Catholic hierarchy . . . is mobilizing powerful forces to move this nation toward a cultural unity in which the Roman Catholic Church will be dominant." It was his opinion that unless some "unity of effort" could be found among Protestants in America to match the unity among Catholics, Catholicism could definitely "win America." [17]

The thought of Catholicism winning the nation, plus some genuine concern among many Protestants over the church-state issue, caused Protestants to continue to protest, even during the war years, the existence of U.S.-Vatican relations. In 1944 the Federal Council of Churches issued a statement openly opposing the establishment of diplomatic relations with the Vatican. [18] In reply, the *Pilot,* official publication of the Boston Catholic archdiocese, supported diplomatic relations and asked the Federal Council not to be afraid of American Catholics. [19] It was evident to many Catholic leaders in America by then that Protestant leaders feared the growing influence of the Catholic church in the country.

Further evidence of the existence of deep interfaith tensions during World War II is seen in the immediate revival of full-scale conflicts after the war. In October 1945 Methodist Bishop G. Bromley Oxnam, then president of the Federal Council of Churches, declared that "serious religious tension is developing between Roman Catholics and Protestants in the United States." [20] The predominant roots of these tensions were the now familiar ones—Protestant suspicion of the new Catholic power and Catholic impatience for recognition as a religious influence in America equal to Protestantism. The postwar conflicts centered on two issues, the Vatican embassy and federal aid to parochial schools. Resolutions by Protestant groups often denounced both at the same time.

The Vatican question was already in the air as the war began drawing to a close. In April 1945 President Harry S. Truman reconfirmed Taylor as presidential representative to the Vatican.[21] In October of that year the New Jersey Baptist Convention gave one of the first of the Protestant postwar outcries by demanding that Taylor be recalled.[22] Undaunted, Truman in May 1946 gave Taylor the rank of ambassador.[23] On the heels of this, in one six-week period, the Executive Committee of the Federal Council of Churches, the Baltimore Conference of the Methodist Church, the General Assembly of the Presbyterian Church, U.S.A., the General Assembly of the Universalist Church, the General Synod of the Reformed Church in America, the Northern Baptist Convention, and the Southern Baptist Convention all adopted resolutions calling for an end to U.S.-Vatican relations.[24] In June 1946 a delegation of Protestant leaders representing denominations with a combined membership of thirty million and led by Samuel McCrea Cavert, general secretary of the Federal Council of Churches, visited Truman and protested the Vatican post as "contrary to the historic American principle of the separation of church and state."[25] The president told the delegation that Taylor's mission was temporary but that it would end only when world peace was firmly established.[26]

As in the period before the war, Protestants' motives for demanding Taylor's recall varied. Among most of them, however, there was a growing fear that the existence of the Vatican embassy would help the Catholic hierarchy to influence the power structures of America to favor Catholicism above all other religious persuasions. The longer the delay in ending the mission to the Vatican the more suspicious of Catholic motives Protestants became. In September 1947 six hundred Protestant laymen and 1,275 Protestant clergymen (including one from England) petitioned the president to end the Vatican embassy, declaring in their petition that the Papacy wished to "rule the world through states subservient to its will."[27] The *Christian Century* ran frequent editorials on the Vatican post, referring on one occasion to Taylor's mission as "a political maneuver to impress American Catholics," and suggesting on another occasion that his appointment reflected intimidation "by Roman Catholic pressure made in full awareness that an election is pending."[28]

Since many of the Protestant reactions came from established Protestant spokesmen rather than irresponsible reactionaries, they were definite indications of the new level of Catholic strength in the country. Only a strong and growing movement could have evoked such a widespread expression of concern among so many different groups of Protestants. Protestants were no longer the unchallenged leaders of American religious life, but rather religion in America was for the first time becoming definitely pluralistic.

Catholics, as well as Protestants, had to adjust to this new pluralism. And just as Protestants in their anxiety often impugned the intentions of Catholics, Catholics in their impatience sometimes impugned the motives of Protestants. An example was the remark of Cardinal Spellman of New York when he called the June 1946 Protestant delegation to the White House "anti-Catholicism of unhooded Klansmen sowing seeds of dissention and disunion."[29]

Also, Catholics began pressing their advantages to the point of aggravating the interfaith conflict. They were, for example, as vociferous as the Protestants in condemning Truman's statement that he would bring Taylor home after peace was established. Whereas the latter objected that it was merely a nebulous promise, Catholics opposed it as a commitment to terminate a desirable post. They used the channels of public pressure in an effort to bring about a permanent Vatican embassy just as Protestants did in attempting to sever all Vatican connections. Organizations such as the Catholic War Veterans of America adopted resolutions urging the appointment of a permanent ambassador to the Papal See[30] at the same time Protestant groups were asking for an end to Taylor's mission. Archbishop James H. Ryan of Omaha called anything less than full diplomatic representation a "sop" to a noisy minority of Protestant leaders.[31] It is doubtful that Catholic groups and Catholic leaders in America were primarily concerned over the existence of a Vatican embassy, however. Rather, the Vatican post was a symbol of their new strength and maturity in American life, and thus when they fought to make the post permanent they were actually fighting to stabilize their influence.

Taylor resigned his position in 1950, and once the president had accepted the resignation one hundred editors of Protestant papers in the United States and Canada thanked Truman for accepting the resignation and begged him to abolish the post entirely.[32] But in 1951 Truman called General Mark W. Clark, chief of the Army Field Forces, into his office and asked him to take the post as full-ranking United States ambassador to the Vatican. General Clark relates that Truman specifically said that he was looking for a Protestant for the post. When Clark, who confesses to being surprised by the president's asking him to take the position, asked Truman if there were someone with whom he could discuss the matter, Truman suggested Myron Taylor, and, said Clark, "I flew that same day to talk with him in New York and he thought I should accept."[33] Clark, like Taylor an Episcopalian, had been in contact with the former presidential representative on several occasions when the United States forces were in Rome during World War II. He had talked with Taylor about his duties "on a good many occasions" but "the religious issue was not discussed at length." "We knew it was there," relates Clark, "but we both felt there should be some representation by the United States at the Vatican in order to have access to the tremendous amount of intelligence which they gathered."[34] Clark testifies that he had not been aware of the religious controversies stirred up by Taylor's appointment and that he was rather surprised by the amount of reaction to the news of his pending appointment, especially by the number of letters he received. Most of the mail, states Clark, "was from Protestant people who dealt with the subject of the separation of church and state."[35] It appears that neither he nor Truman, nor political leaders generally, were aware of the intensity of the suspicions between Protestants and Catholics in the country. But because interfaith tensions were so strong it would have been impossible for Truman or Clark or anyone else to confine the question of a Vatican embassy to the political arena.

The Catholic hierarchy betrayed its vested concern for a

Vatican embassy by immediate and forthright endorsement of Clark's appointment. Archbishop Cushing of Boston called the news "a joyful announcement" and declared that "it means the recognition of the Vatican state as one of the greatest international forces for the defeat of Communism on a world-wide basis."[36] In equally emphatic language Cardinal Spellman stated: "Certainly the United States and the Holy See have identical objectives of peace, and it is most logical therefore that there should be a practical exchange of viewpoints in search for this peace."[37]

Protestant opposition, on the other hand, was so widespread that newspaper accounts could hardly keep up with it. On the same day that the *New York Times* announced the appointment of Clark, the newspaper carried quotations of fourteen Protestant leaders, some heads of national Protestant bodies, opposing the appointment. Included was the statement of Episcopal Bishop Henry Knox Sherill, president of the recently formed National Council of Churches, who said: "I hope and believe this unwise proposal will be opposed by the great majority of fair-minded Americans of every religious conviction."[38] Soon the National Council released a lengthy official statement on the Vatican embassy question. While repudiating religious prejudice and dissention, the statement declared that "the appointment of an Ambassador to the Vatican would be wrong in principle, useless in practice and would produce consequences both far reaching and disastrous to the national unity of the American people."[39] The National Council urged the president to withdraw the appointment at once so as to avoid a far-reaching controversy in the country. Then in terse language the statement read: "We did not choose this controversy. We deplore it. But we cannot and will not evade it. We have been in the past and will continue to be in the future unalterably opposed to the establishment of diplomatic relations with the Vatican."[40] The General Board of the National Council soon organized a nationwide campaign of protest spearheaded by leaders in several Protestant denominations in the country.[41]

It became quite difficult for either Protestant or Catholic

spokesmen to stick to the subject of the Vatican embassy. Bishop G. Bromley Oxnam of the Methodist church declared in the *Nation* in November 1951 that "the American people will not be led down the road to Rome." [42] On the other hand, the *Catholic News*, official publication of the New York archdiocese, called opponents of the embassy "professional anti-Catholics." [43] In truth, neither Protestants nor Catholics could at this point think clearly about the issues. The question of the Vatican embassy had been around for over a decade by then and had been kept alive and burning all that time. Both sides were weary of the conflict, but each was afraid to stop for fear of being overrun by the other.

In January 1952, when the controversy was at its peak, Clark asked Truman to withdraw his name. The general gave, as one reason, his military status, indicating personal conflict over whether he should resign from the Army if he accepted the position of ambassador.[44] In private correspondence after his retirement, he maintained that the vote on ratification of his appointment was scheduled so close to Senate adjournment that it amounted to a "recess appointment, which I could not accept." [45] It is hard to believe, however, that the public controversy over church-state relations in connection with his Vatican assignment had nothing to do with his asking for release, especially since Clark himself testifies that he was surprised by the public reaction.[46]

While the conflict over the Vatican embassy was going on, the parochial school controversy was also in full swing. Either one in itself would have been sufficient to fan the flames of interfaith misunderstandings. Both together made Protestant-Catholic relations in America seem irreparably broken.

The parochial school controversy was actually more intense than the Vatican embassy question. Whereas the majority of Americans had never seen the Vatican, the question of public aid to parochial schools was quite close to home. It involved not just a corporation executive or an Army general but people's own children and those of their neighbors.

The question of parochial versus public education had been

around for quite some time. It had given rise to a legal controversy in the 1920s when two cases reached the Supreme Court. In *Meyer* v. *Nebraska* in 1923, the Supreme Court struck down a Nebraska act prohibiting the teaching of foreign languages prior to the eighth grade in both public and private schools. Though the test case had concerned a Lutheran school, the issue affected more Roman Catholic schools than any others because of the large number of Catholic schools in the country. The Court's decision was a reaffirmation of freedom for the parochial school system.[47] In *Pierce* v. *Society of the Sisters of the Holy Name of Jesus and Mary*, in 1925, the Supreme Court ruled against a 1922 Oregon law which had outlawed parochial elementary education in the state, contending that the due-process clause of the Fourteenth Amendment made the religious guarantees of the First Amendment binding on state as well as federal government.[48]

Taken together, the two decisions had sanctioned both the existence and autonomy of parochial education in America. However, the financing of this education was another matter. Here there were deep divisions. Protestants, generally, asserted that any support of parochial schools or of parochial school children with public funds violated the separation of church and state. Catholics, however, declared it their right as American citizens to receive government support for the education of their children just as did people in the public schools.

To a degree, the inflation after World War II seems to have accentuated the conflict. Parochial education without the benefit of public funds was hard-pressed financially. Receiving additional money from the coffers of the various levels of government would have relieved some of the budgetary pressures Catholic school leaders were feeling. But since inflation was no respecter of church affiliation, Protestants were of no mind to support two school systems at once. The argument that this is precisely what Catholics were doing carried no weight for Protestants, for the latter declared that Catholics had freely chosen to establish parochial schools and should therefore bear the full responsibility for them.

However, the arguments from both sides never stayed in the realm of finances. The debates moved, instead, into questions of motive, each side often accusing the other of conniving or bigotry. At root, then, the parochial school controversy was not a financial hassle. Mutual feelings of distrust and animosity had simply grown stronger, especially with the question over an embassy at the Vatican in the air, and no amount of financial security could have kept Protestants from fearing Catholic power or Catholics from forceful self-assertion. The fact that Catholics gave no real emphasis to the receipt of aid by non-Catholic parochial schools is significant. Had their concern been primarily one of public aid to parochial schools as a matter of principle, they would have stressed receipt by non-Catholic schools more strongly. But because Catholics spoke almost exclusively in terms of their own schools, one is led to conclude that they were asserting themselves *as Catholics*—another expression of American Catholicism's coming of age.

The conflict gained momentum early in 1947 when the Supreme Court in *Everson* v. *Board of Education*, by a 5-to-4 decision, upheld a New Jersey law permitting parochial school children to ride public school buses. The *Christian Century* mirrored Protestant reaction by declaring that the "ultimate purpose" of Roman Catholicism was "to shift to the public treasury the entire burden of financing its parochial schools while the church retains control of the educational process in them." "Protestantism can no longer be complacent in the face of such encroachments by the Roman Church," declared the editors.[49] It was the bell sounding the beginning of another round in the fight between the two religious establishments.

This round, like the others, was filled with accusations and name-calling. The Council of Bishops of the Methodist church called the decision "a serious threat to our public education system which is the bulwark of democracy."[50] The *Commonweal* accused Protestants of having "anti-Vatican hysteria,"[51] and Cardinal Spellman charged that a new anti-Catholic bigotry comparable to that in the Al Smith campaign was afoot in America.[52]

A prime example of the intensified conflict took place in North College Hill, a Cincinnati, Ohio, suburb. Tensions had existed there as far back as 1940 when there was a proposal that the Catholic parochial school become part of the public school system. Reaction to this brought on the election of a substantial Protestant majority to the school board the following year. Two years later, 1943, this board hired William A. Cook as superintendent of schools. In the 1945 school board election Catholics regained the majority in a campaign divided along religious lines. Conflict between the new board and Dr. Cook resulted in the board's refusal to renew the superintendent's contract, which was to expire in the summer of 1947. Emotions had risen so high in the community by this time that a school strike resulted, bringing about an investigation by the National Education Association. The NEA demanded Cook's retention and blacklisted the school system when the school board refused to comply.[53] According to Cook's own testimony, it was the first time NEA had ever moved into a local situation to protect personnel.[54] After a series of brawls and riots, the school board resigned *en masse*, and Cook, who over twenty years later still referred to the Catholic members as "those fellows,"[55] was reinstated.[56] The NEA in its investigation report wrote: "Probably the most unfortunate consequence arising out of the North College Hill situation has been the marked spread of and increase in tension between certain members of the Catholic and Protestant faiths."[57] Evidence of this was the fact that the Cincinnati Council of Churches conducted its own investigation.[58]

Throughout the entire wartime and postwar period, the school question in the country remained a front. The real issue was not education but religious power. Evidence of this is seen in the nationwide sectarian division over two aid-to-education bills introduced in Congress in the postwar 1940s.

The first, sponsored by Senator Robert A. Taft of Ohio, in 1947, called for federal funds to the states, with the states deciding whether the money would be used to aid parochial as well as public schools.[59] Hardly had the bill been proposed when Protestants and Catholics around the country entered into fierce debate over the bill's merit. It is doubtful that any bill proposed by Congress had ever caused as much clearcut division of opinion between Protestants and Catholics on a nationwide scale. Sometimes both groups opposed the measure but for different reasons—Protestants because it made federal aid to parochial schools possible and Catholics because the bill did not guarantee it.[60] Significant is the fact that neither group paid much attention to the provision for aid to public schools, though this provision was itself a new concept. Had the issue really been education, more discussion would have taken place over the question of federal aid itself. But the attention of religious leaders stayed glued to the parochial school question, with Catholics emphasizing only what Catholics should get and Protestants declaring that they should not get anything. Of special significance is the fact that in the heavily Protestant South, the idea of states' rights, which the South was voicing louder and louder by 1947, was not a live issue when the merits of the Taft bill were debated. Though the Ohio senator's proposal made the states the guardians of the funds, the Southern Protestants still supported national efforts to stop the bill.[61]

The Taft bill, and a similar one by Senator George Aiken of Vermont, passed the Senate in 1948, but both of them died in the House of Representatives.[62] Undoubtedly, religious pressure had something to do with the death of the bills. Samuel McCrea Cavert, general secretary of the Federal Council of Churches, and representatives of the National Association of Evangelicals, the Congregational Christian churches, and the Methodist church all testified against the bills before a House subcommittee hearing.[63] Another bill, though, introduced in the House in 1949 by Representative Graham Barden, kept the debates alive. The Barden bill differed from the Taft and Aiken measures in that it specifically confined the aid to public schools.[64]

A great reversal of positions from those on the Taft bill took place, but once more the positions were drawn along sectarian lines. Protestants rallied behind the Barden bill's support, and

Catholics organized a massive crusade against it. The 1949 Southern Baptist Convention endorsed the bill, and the New York State Council of Churches applauded the bill's limitation clause as being "in the public interest." [65] Conversely, posters describing the bill as "unjust, un-American, and divisive" were displayed in St. Patrick's Cathedral in New York.[66] Cardinal Spellman called Barden "a new disciple of bigotry" and those in Congress who supported the bill "disciples of discrimination." [67]

The interfaith conflict over the Barden bill was further evidence of the primary concern over matters other than government financing of education. Had Protestant people in America been concerned only with the question of school aid, they would not have rallied en masse behind the Barden bill. It is very difficult to assume such unilateral political persuasion on the merits of federal aid to education alone, especially when this idea was itself new. But the bill did afford the occasion for showing the fast-growing bid among Catholics for more voice in American education, and on this, Protestants were united.

For Catholics it was a question of government recognition of their existence. They had grown to the point where they felt it the duty of the society to recognize them, and a logical way to do this was for the public to give due support to the Catholic schools and school children in the country. Reservations by Catholics over the Taft proposal because it did not guarantee aid to parochial schools was evidence of this thirst for recognition. When the Barden bill specifically denied aid to their schools, Catholics in America took it as a personal affront. Their bids for federal aid to parochial schools in essence represented a Catholic liberation movement in America. In a liberation movement, participants often demand recognition at the expense of benefits to others not among them. So it was in the massive Catholic resistance to the Barden bill. Nothing in Catholic dogma would have called for massive resistance to a bill providing aid to public schools. But if Catholics were not to receive aid, they were determined that no one else would either. After the Barden bill died in committee, largely be-

cause of the religious impasse, Methodist Bishop Bromley Oxnam declared in a radio interview which was entered into the
Congressional Record by Congressman Tom Steed of Oklahoma
that "the Roman Catholic hierarchy is responsible for killing
the bills that might have brought Federal aid to our public
school system."[68]

In essence, both religious establishments were responsible
for helping bring about the defeat of federal aid to education
during the late 1940s. That an interfaith conflict could halt
congressional legislation is itself evidence of the scope and intensity of Catholic-Protestant discord. Catholic and Protestant
alike were intransigent on the school question because each
feared the power of the other.

Bishop Oxnam's statement in the *Congressional Record* did,
perhaps unwittingly, reflect a root cause of the conflict by its
tacit admission that Roman Catholicism had reached a new
level of influence in America. Protestantism could no longer
maintain an unchallenged leadership in the religious influence
on politics and society in America. This was a frightening development to many Protestants and one to which they had a
difficult time adjusting. The intensity of the parochial school
issue, therefore, demonstrated the existence of a new pluralism
in American religious life. America was no longer Protestant
plus Catholic, but Protestant and Catholic.

It was largely because of the difficulty in adjusting to the new
pluralism that an organization calling itself by the imposing
title Protestants and Other Americans United for the Separation
of Church and State was born. The adoption of the name "Protestants" indicates the significant assumption held by its found-
ers that American Protestantism was generally united in concern
over a growing Catholic monolith in the country. Because of this
assumption of nationwide support, the organization became
hyperaggressive in its efforts to keep down Catholic influence
in public life in general.

Plans for a nationwide organization had existed since 1946.
According to William A. Cook of North College Hill fame, it
was the North College Hill case of 1947, though, which brought

about definite action.[69] In November of that year sixty leaders in church, educational, and fraternal circles adopted a manifesto called "Separation of Church and State," and POAU (as the organization referred to itself) became an official establishment.

The manifesto contained a long section describing Roman Catholic efforts to obtain government aid for parochial schools (including a criticism of the Taft bill) and accusing the Catholic hierarchy of political pressure concerning the Vatican embassy. It then listed some "immediate objectives." Here the writers struck hard against any public aid for church schools, free textbooks for parochial school use, or free transportation for parochial school pupils and urged "all patriotic citizens" to join hands to prevent Congress from appropriating funds to church-supported education. The manifesto demanded an end to "the ambassadorship to the papal head of the Roman Catholic Church." It also pledged "to enlighten and mobilize public opinion in support of religious liberty." [70]

So strong were the fears and feelings motivating POAU that the organization could barely deny being anti-Catholic. "As Protestants we can be called anti-Catholic only in the sense in which every Catholic is anti-Protestant," stated the manifesto.[71] Through their omission here of any reference to "Other Amercans" POAU's principal spokesmen gave evidence that they conceived of their organization in at least a quasi-ecclesiastical sense. In fact, William Cook of the North College Hill case, who later affiliated with POAU, testified that Charles Clayton Morrison and Joseph Dawson, both POAU leaders, objected strongly to the move which came some years later to drop the term "Protestant" from the name.[72] Furthermore, the manifesto's specificity in naming the Roman Catholic Church as an agent whose actions they opposed, a choice obviously taken in preference to the common procedure of referring to groups opposed in the abstract, indicated a determination on the part of POAU to deal in corporate personalities as well as in principle.

By mid-1948 POAU had begun a periodical called *Church and State*, which in its first issue was filled with references to

Catholic power in America. Among the periodical's concerns was the fact that though Catholics numbered only one-sixth of the voting population, they had the second largest number of members in the House of Representatives. Though the Senate was over eight-to-one Protestant, the editors of *Church and State* lamented "too little evidence of Protestant conviction" in the Senate.[73] In July of 1948, POAU named Glenn L. Archer, then dean of the Law School of Washburn University in Topeka, Kansas, national director of the organization.[74]

In Catholic circles POAU was anathema. The National Catholic Welfare Conference charged the signers of the manifesto with "strange and utterly un-American mentality."[75] The Knights of Columbus asserted that POAU had impugned the patriotism of "any citizen, Catholic, Jew, Protestant, or nonbeliever who dares to disagree with the organization's biased and inaccurate interpretation of the First Amendment."[76] Cardinal Spellman appeared before a public meeting in Rochester, New York, to protest the new organization and Archbishop Richard Cushing hinted that communist sympathy existed among its leaders.[77]

The birth of POAU epitomized the main distinction between the Protestant reaction to Catholic growth in the 1920s and Protestant reaction to the new religious pluralism of the 1940s. In the former case, a nonecclesiastically based reactionary leadership, often lacking extensive formal education, gave rise to physical force in groups such as the Ku Klux Klan. In the latter case an ecclesiastically oriented, highly educated leadership, skilled with words and phrases, brought about a manifesto and an apparently sophisticated organization. In essence, POAU was a nationwide admission that Catholicism had gained enormous strength in America and was fast becoming an influence equal to that of Protestantism. Had POAU's leaders felt otherwise, they would never have founded the organization in the first place.

While POAU was in its early days of formation and operation, Paul Blanshard, a former State Department official, entered the picture and further intensified the interfaith conflicts in America. On his own initiative, he published an article in the *Nation*, followed, upon request of the magazine, by more, on the Catholic church.[78] Not a Catholic himself, Blanshard fiercely denounced what he said was the official position of the Catholic hierarchy regarding medicine, sex, and education.[79] Though himself an ordained clergyman, a fact few people, either Protestant or Catholic, seemed to know, Blanshard, who years later seemed rather defensive about his efforts,[80] asserted that he "deliberately omitted any claim to clerical expertness at the time simply because I wanted to write from a nonclerical point of view about social policies of the Church rather than its religious dogma."[81]

Blanshard's articles amounted to a scathing denunciation of the whole authoritarian structure of Roman Catholicism. The Jesuit journal *America* referred to them as a "smear smut."[82] In Newark, New Jersey, upon request of Catholic parents and the recommendation of the director of school libraries, Superintendent John V. Herron banned the *Nation* from four high schools in the city.[83] The result was a hearing in which Blanshard himself testified, "speaking in general for free speech and also criticising the Catholic birth control theories."[84] Shortly afterward, Blanshard wrote another series of articles for the *Nation* denouncing Catholic practices, this time the result being a ban of the magazine in New York City.[85] For the better part of a month pulpits resounded with sermons on the ban, Catholics defending it, Protestants generally attacking it.[86] From these experiences, Blanshard went on to produce a book called *American Freedom and Catholic Power* and in the prologue stated: "Unfortunately the Catholic people in the United States are not citizens but *subjects* in their own religious commonwealth."[87]

At some other time in American history Blanshard's work might have been passed over as the work of a man who simply had a bone to pick. That his work received great public attention is simply further demonstration of the national scope of Protestant-Catholic tensions during the late 1940s and early 1950s. Given the momentum of Catholic influence during this period and the questions it lodged in the minds of many educated Protestants, as well as others, it was almost inevitable that sooner or later someone of non-Catholic persuasion would come along to write objections about this influence and warnings to the American people. Though they intensified the conflict, Blanshard's writings were more the result of interfaith struggles already going on. Instead of presenting something really new to the American people, Blanshard mainly gathered up and reflected the fears and anxieties of the non-Catholic America which had become overwhelmed by the new power of the Catholic church in the nation and which was for the first time affected in all phases of its life by that church.

It was also inevitable that a body experiencing such rapid growth of influence as the Catholic church in America should see itself in a special light once its influence reached a level comparable to that of others. An article appearing in the *Catholic World* early in 1948 gave explicit expression to this new self-image. Its title was "Catholic America Comes of Age." The major point of the article was striking. It asserted simply that Catholic leadership in the world now centered in America rather than in Europe and that American Catholicism should feel a new sense of responsibility for the future. The responsibility included both steering the Catholic forces throughout the world and thoroughly propagating the Catholic faith in America.[88]

These two goals of being the world leader of Catholicism and making converts in the United States were the major motives of American Catholicism during the 1940s and early 1950s. In order to secure its new-found leadership in world affairs, the Catholic church of America desired a place of influence in the land of the world political leaders. Feeling, because of the earlier history of Protestant-Catholic struggles in the country, that it would not evolve to this level of influence automatically, the Catholic church pushed itself at every point where she saw new glimmers of recognition. In doing so she shocked Protestant America, which had become accustomed to a dominant role in American religious life. The unexpected advent of American political presence at the Vatican in 1939 had taken American Protestantism aback, and the growing problem of parochial and public education, coming as it did on the heels of this, made the Protestant establishment in America ever more suspicious of Catholic advances and ever more defensive of its own spheres of influence. The entire clash of the 1940s and early 1950s was the result of a religious body with a new self-image and an established religious body with an accustomed role of leadership meeting in the same place at the same time. Out of this clash, America moved from a Protestant-oriented society to a nation of definite religious pluralism, so that by 1955 Will Herberg could write in *Protestant-Catholic-Jew* of "a strong sense of self-assurance" among Catholics in America and could say: "Protestantism is no longer identical with America. . . . Protestantism has, in fact, become merely one of three communions (or communities) with equal status and equal legitimacy in the American scheme of things." [89]

III.

Toward Relationships of Maturity: 1955-1967

Few people thought in 1950 that Protestant-Catholic relations in America would ever be anything but tense and hostile. Groups such as the National Conference of Christians and Jews were still functioning, but the public consciousness had buried them beneath the barrage of interfaith conflicts which had fallen on America. POAU still warned Americans of what POAU said were Catholic ambitions to control the country. Catholic leaders such as Cardinal Spellman still echoed their angry outbursts toward Protestants who opposed a Vatican embassy or federal aid to parochial schools. Even the McCarthy hearings fanned the flames of conflict with accusations by one of the Catholic senator's associates that "the largest single group supporting the Communist apparatus in the United States today is composed of Protestant clergymen." [1]

But sometimes the most turbulent situations have within them the seeds of their own improvement. People do get tired of controversy. It had been so in 1928 after the campaign of Al Smith, when NCCJ was born. It was becoming the case again by the mid-1950s. In 1953 one of America's leading Protestant figures, Reinhold Niebuhr, wrote an article for the *Commonweal* under the assigned title "A Protestant Looks at Catholics," but which in reality dealt with Protestant-Catholic relations.

Near the conclusion of the article, Niebuhr wrote the following words:

> I must apologize for considering the problem of Catholic-Protestant
> relations in this article rather than the exact theme which the editor
> assigned to me. This was done because of a pressing personal concern
> about the absence of any genuine community between us, and the
> conviction that the inevitable frictions between religious groups and
> churches will breed mistrust, fear, and even hatred if there is no effort
> to eliminate misunderstandings.[2]

By 1955, similar sentiment was being expressed more and
more often in American religious journalism. Especially significant was an editorial in the October 19, 1955, issue of the
Christian Century calling for an end to what the writer called
Catholic claustrophobia and Protestant paranoia. The former
was the feeling of Catholics that they must fight aggressively
on every front in order to attain status and to keep from being
closed off by a Protestant society; the latter was the tendency
for Protestants to be threatened by any Roman Catholic activity.[3] Two months later the *Catholic World* responded to the
Christian Century editorial with praise and called for American
Catholics to "renounce our pet prejudices, our historical scape-
goats, sweeping generalizations about Protestants, name-calling
and gossip."[4]

A prime example of the changing attitudes in America is
found in the decline in prestige of POAU during the middle
and later 1950s. This organization had enjoyed reasonable endorsement by American Protestants since its inception. But by
1955 there were evident differences of emphasis between POAU
and the National Council of Churches, especially when the
latter contended that there was a place for the teaching of religion in a child's curriculum.[5] Furthermore, no one had been
named to a Vatican embassy post since Mark Clark's withdrawal
in 1952, and no major federal aid to education bill had been
introduced in Congress since the death of the Barden bill in
1949. POAU had thrived on these issues, but the passing of time
had lessened their intensity in the public mind. Without a

specific target of national interest the organization began picking at much smaller matters and began to appear blatantly negative.[6] The cardinal event in its loss of support came in 1957 when POAU asked the Federal Communications Commission to refuse television licenses to St. Louis University and Loyola University of New Orleans, both Jesuit schools, on the grounds that the Jesuit order was alien and therefore ineligible for TV licenses.[7] When POAU's director, Glenn Archer, explained the action as "part of a counterattack against the sectarian pressure which has caused the banning of the film *Martin Luther* by a Chicago TV station"[8] some leaders in America's Protestant community had all they could take. In an editorial in *Christianity and Crisis*, Robert McAfee Brown, then a professor at Union Theological Seminary in New York, labeled POAU's counterattack "Protestantism reduced to anti-Catholicism" and called for Protestants in America "to disassociate themselves in large numbers from an organization so ill-equipped to speak in their name."[9] In a short time, dissassociations did come from various quarters. Early in 1958 the Connecticut Council of Churches publicly disavowed any connections with POAU.[10] In the same year John M. Krumm, Protestant chaplain at Columbia, charged the organization with "doing enormous harm to the cause of co-operation and understanding between Protestants and Roman Catholics by its exaggerated definition of the Church-State principle."[11] These remarks were in part precipitated by a POAU effort to keep American cardinals from voting in the election of a new Pope on the grounds that a 1952 Immigration and Naturalization Act said that a citizen voting in an election in a foreign state would lose his citizenship.[12] Of particular embarrassment to POAU was the resignation of one of its own leading "other Americans," Stanley Lichtenstein, a Jewish proponent of church-state separation, in protest of a POAU publication containing "Questions for a Catholic Candidate," which, said Lichtenstein, violated the no-religious-test clause of Article Six of the Constitution.[13] Time was turning against POAU by the later 1950s, for instead of wanting to keep alive the issues of the late 1940s and early 1950s, leaders from many religious persuasions were anxious to develop more affirmative and mature interfaith contacts.

The reactions of the middle and late 1950s to interfaith negativism had in them some dimensions not found in the reactions of the 1930s to the conflicts of the 1920s. Most significant was the absence of a specific national event of interfaith focus during the mid-1950s. There was no presidential campaign involving a Roman Catholic around which to rally a theme of good will. This made the movement toward improvement of relations stronger. Once a specific major event fades into the background, the efforts and attitudes springing from it tend also to diminish. But when there is no one special event to fade, movements toward improved attitudes can build on their own positive foundations. The movement of the mid-1950s was this way. It was a movement whose time had come; it was more than a reaction to specific unpleasantries. Religious America simply had had time by the middle to later 1950s to adjust to new pluralism, and thoughtful leaders from both Catholic and Protestant circles were anxious to see that the interfaith relations of the two leading religious establishments be responsible and mature ones. Thurston N. Davis, S.J., editor of *America*, expressed this feeling in 1957 when he prepared an address for CBS's "Church of the Air" radio program advocating open and thoughtful discussions of Catholic-Protestant tensions. When the network canceled the address because it was not devotional in nature, the Jesuit priest published it in his own periodical,[14] whereupon the *Christian Century* responded with an equal desire for improved relationships by calling for "adult discussion of religion on radio."[15] Responsible and mature interfaith relations were being seen more and more as those which expressed the deeper, more harmonious, and transforming characteristics of religion rather than bickerings and discord based on partial understandings.

Indication of newly developing attitudes is seen in the appearance of three significant books during the same year, 1955. One of these was *The Catholic Approach to Protestantism* by George H. Tavard, a French priest living and working in

America. Tavard relates that he wrote it at the suggestion of a professor in a Spanish university who wished to strengthen the ecumenical movement in Spain. But the "reason behind the book," says the author, "was my own interest in Christian unity. I was working at the time on my more scholarly volume, *Holy Writ or Holy Church,* and I was anxious to do something that could have also a more popular appeal and impact."[16] Tavard's interest in unity was strong enough for him to make his own English translation from the French original. (It was never published in Spanish.)[17] He briefly reviewed Reformation history and Protestant doctrines and suggested that Protestant and Catholic themes were sometimes closer than either side realized. Out of this he called for interfaith relationships based on theological understanding instead of just on polemics.[18] It was the first forthright irenic writing on Protestant-Catholic relations to appear on the American religious scene during the entire period since World War I. A reviewer in the *Commonweal* wrote: "This book may open a new era in our relationship with what we call our 'separated brethren,' "[19] and a reviewer in the *Christian Century* wrote that the book could help Catholic and Protestant "both to stand a little straighter under God and behave more like decent human beings toward each other."[20] The affirmative response by both groups to the book was as indicative as the appearance of the book itself that a desire for new attitudes in interfaith circles was in the air.

A second book appearing the same year dealt directly with the interfaith scene in America. It was *Catholic-Protestant Conflicts in America* by John J. Kane, chairman of the Sociology Department at Notre Dame. The book marked the first major attempt by either a Protestant or a Catholic writer to make an objective analysis of the complexities of Protestant-Catholic interaction in the United States. Kane's desire for improved relationships was expressed when he called the elimination of conflicts a "milestone almost in sight" and concluded that not only American Catholics but "millions of American Protestants" longed for an end to the conflicts.[21]

The third book to appear in 1955 had the special significance of being written by an American Jew. It was Will Herberg's classic treatise on American religious sociology, *Protestant-Catholic-Jew*. From the perspective of religious life in America generally, Herberg certainly wrote as one from within, but his remarks on both American Catholicism and American Protestantism had an appearance of objectivity simply because he was a member of neither but an observer of both. His mention of a "strong sense of self-assurance" among Catholics and of Protestantism's being "no longer identical with America" helped readers from both groups to recognize more clearly the new pluralism which American religion was experiencing.[22] Both the Catholic and the Protestant press gave a good bit of attention to the book[23] and by this indicated that at least to some extent each was willing to accept and build on the new patterns of religious influence and power that were present in the nation.

Once the new patterns had been recognized and accepted by leaders in both Catholic and Protestant communities, the concern for religious dialogue and better mutual understanding became a movement in itself. The strength of the movement this time lay in the presence of that dimension which had been notably absent in the brotherhood days of the 1930s—theological concern. The lack of a specific national political event to create a religious issue during the middle and later 1950s was itself a factor making possible more open consideration of religious doctrines *per se*. This was a fortunate state of affairs, for conflicts between religious establishments are never simply political matters. Even the parochial school issue had had a theological dimension. Traditional Roman Catholic ecclesiology had considered education to be basically a function of the church, whereas in most Protestant circles there was a more tightly defined view of the church as a body called apart for specific tasks of worship and service with education not being a primary church function. In other words, Protestants simply held a more separatist view of what the church was in society than did Catholics. In the early 1940s, when the question of public support of parochial education was strongest, neither Protestant nor Catholic in America had really recognized the theological dimensions of their conflict. This had weakened the possibility of any deeper mutual understanding of why each group advocated what it did and had made a peaceable settlement just that much less likely.

Foundations were being laid for less frenzied discussions of numerous social issues, therefore, once the doctrinal positions of each body were made more open. By 1957 evidence of this new theological openness was clearly present. In that year a project called "Operation Understanding" initiated in Belleville, Illinois, by bishops of the Catholic diocese brought Catholics and Protestants, both lay and clerical, together in information sessions on each other's beliefs and modes of worship.[24] In the same year, a Lutheran-sponsored institute of Roman Catholic studies began operations in Minneapolis for the purpose of studying Catholic theology.[25] Thus in one calendar year both Catholic and Protestant groups in America had taken the initiative in organizing depth study of doctrinal issues. This new spirit of inquiry showed a definite desire for better understanding of one another and hence a desire for better relations. This in turn reflected a new stage of development in American religious life, one in which Catholic and Protestant alike were recognizing the definite and permanent presence of religious pluralism in the nation; each was more readily acknowledging the right of the other to exist and to propagate its own views.

Further evidence of these newer attitudes occurred when, also in 1957, two prominent Roman Catholic observers attended the Protestant-oriented North American Faith and Order Study Conference at Oberlin College. The observers, John B. Sheerin, C.S.P., editor of the *Catholic World*, and Gustave Weigel, S.J., from the faculty of Woodstock College School of Divinity in Maryland, far from being regarded as spies from an enemy camp were welcomed as respected guests. In turn, both of them wrote favorably about the conference, not just in terms of hospitality but in terms of theological concern as well.[26]

During the next two years, Protestant-Catholic dialogue continued at an increasing pace along many avenues of concern. The entire June 1959 issue of *Christianity and Crisis* was devoted to interfaith conversation about political and sociological matters with references to Catholic and Protestant ideologies and theological viewpoints as well.[27] All this prompted the Jesuit publication *America* to note: "There is no denying that the long-awaited dialog between American Catholics and Protestants has at last begun."[28]

Indication that it had begun came on even stronger in 1959 with the publication of *The Riddle of Roman Catholicism* by Jaroslav Pelikan, an American Protestant and then a professor of historical theology at the University of Chicago. Written primarily for Protestant readers, the book aimed at a theological understanding of both traditions in light of one another. This amounted to a real breakthrough in American interfaith patterns, for it was the first time in modern interfaith history that an American Protestant of such scholarly stature had written a basically doctrinal analysis of Protestant-Catholic interaction. In a concluding section the author discussed both "The Unity We Have" and "The Unity We Seek" as Protestants and Catholics.[29] Talk of unity on any front would have been thought unrealistic just a decade earlier when the social and political conflicts involving religious interests were so much in evidence. It was doubly significant, therefore, that Pelikan spoke not only of unity but spoke of it in theological or doctrinal contexts. The presence of these contexts indicated that interfaith concerns were moving not only beyond the conflicts of the 1940s and early 1950s but also beyond the good-will emphases of the 1930s which for the sake of harmony had ruled out discussions of theology.

The new interfaith relationships which were developing in the later 1950s, then, cannot be seen as reactions to the conflicts of the 1940s to mid-1950s in the same sense in which the interfaith styles of the 1930s were reactions to the conflicts of the 1920s. The pattern of interfaith relationships was not that of a pendulum. It was a pattern which followed the definite growth patterns of American Catholicism. When the Catholic church in America reached a stage of development which made her stability and influence largely equal to that of Protestant- ism, the inner life of each group, its doctrinal presuppositions, was of more definite concern to the other. For now, simply an analysis of external manifestations of strength would not solve the abiding interfaith problems.

Another landmark in the developing irenic interfaith pat- terns occurred in 1960 when Robert McAfee Brown and Gus- tave Weigel published their joint work, *An American Dialogue*. The idea of a book written jointly by a Catholic and a Protes- tant had come from Will Herberg, a Jew, whose own recent writings in *Protestant-Catholic-Jew* on America's new religious pluralism were by then widely known. Herberg first approached Weigel about the idea, and Weigel, definitely enthusiastic about such a project, suggested Brown as the Protestant writer. In Brown's words, "Weigel suggested me because he had seen a review I had written of an earlier book of his, in which I had engaged in a certain amount of criticism as well as positive approval, and he thought this would make a good contribu- tion."[30] Each man wrote seven chapters—Brown under the head- ing "A Protestant Looks at Catholicism," and Weigel under the heading "A Catholic Looks at Protestantism." Each man spent much time discussing not only social and political questions but specific theological perspectives of the other tradition, all in a spirit of charity, which was itself a remarkable departure from the standard interfaith comments of five or ten years earlier. Each man called for a genuine religious commitment in each tradition rather than just a commitment to "the American way."[31] This, too, was a departure from the usual emphases involving interfaith interaction, which had focused on themes such as the economic welfare of the nation, as in the case of the brotherhood movement, or constitutional questions such as church and state, as had been the case in the conflicts of the 1940s and early 1950s. It reflected a growing belief that at root questions of interfaith relations were questions of religious and doctrinal outlook and that any lasting solution to inter- faith tensions must be found at the level of theology and doctrine. This growing belief was the result of an adjustment which religious America was making to its pluralistic nature. The authors so much as admitted this when they stated that in America there was a unique opportunity to advance the world-wide theological dialogue because of this unique pluralistic nature which had emerged on America's religious scene.[32] In essence, this was saying America for the good of religion, not religion for the good of America, another example of how improvement in interfaith relationships was transpiring more in ecclesiastical and less in political contexts.

Of course, the whole area of political concern in Catholic-Protestant relations came up again during the presidential campaign of 1960. This time the nomination of Roman Catholic John Fitzgerald Kennedy by the Democratic party brought the question of Catholic dogma and the American Constitution into the open once more.

Much has been written about the religious issue in the 1960 campaign and what it may have signified about Catholicism and the national consciousness by that time. One factor is often overlooked, however; namely, the very nomination of Kennedy itself implied a growing feeling among politicians that the nation's interfaith relationships had improved. Political expediency, always a factor in selecting candidates, would have dictated some other choice than Kennedy had the observers and analysts really felt that the religious issue was still too hot. After the decisive defeat of Al Smith in 1928, many American people had felt that a Roman Catholic could not be elected president of the United States, and this feeling had lingered for years after that. Even as late as 1956, when Kennedy's bid for the vice-presidential nomination failed, there was still evidence of a feeling that a Catholic on the ticket would simply be too great a risk.[33] Four years later the successful elevation of the same man to the presidential nomination demonstrated that the interfaith climate had changed enough for the risk not to seem so great.

Kennedy himself was extremely careful not to make Al Smith's mistake of trying to ignore the question of religion.

Instead, he insisted on keeping it in the open. One of his big steps was to enlist James W. Wine, an associate general secretary of the National Council of Churches, as campaign community relations director.[34] This itself was in stark contrast to the appointment Al Smith had made of John J. Raskob, a Roman Catholic, to the key position of Democratic national chairman in 1928. An acquaintance of Kennedy for several years prior to 1960, Wine testifies to having "talked with him several times about the implications of Catholicism upon his bid for the Presidency with particular reference to how the matter would be received in the national Protestant community."[35] When the Democratic candidate invited him "to take the responsibility for the religious issue in the campaign" Wine resigned his position with the National Council of Churches in order to devote full attention to the task. He accompanied Kennedy as an adviser on various campaign trips, oversaw the correspondence and communications which were related to the question of religion, made arrangements for personal appearances before various groups in the country, and "organized groups to combat the issue in 37 states."[36]

In addition to Wine's efforts, Kennedy himself chose to speak openly on the religious question. His most forthright confrontation of the topic came in Houston, Texas, in mid-September, when he spoke specifically on the issue to the Greater Houston Ministerial Association. This was a body composed predominantly of clergymen of various Protestant orientations. Many of them were of the strongly conservative type, which was the most prone of all to harbor fears of Catholic influence. Both in his prepared speech and in his answers to questions Kennedy emphasized his belief "in an America where the separation of church and state are absolute." Among the most forceful of his comments were the following remarks:

I believe in an America that is officially neither Catholic, Protestant, nor Jewish—where no public official either requests or accepts instruction on public policy from the Pope, the National Council of Churches or any other ecclesiastical source—where no religious body seeks to impose its will directly or indirectly upon the general pop-

ulace or the public acts of its officials—and where religious liberty is
so indivisible that an act against one church is treated as an act
against all.

For a while this year it may be a Catholic against whom the finger
of suspicion is pointed; in other years it has been, and may someday
be again, a Jew—or a Quaker—or a Unitarian—or a Baptist. It was
Virginia's harassment of Baptist preachers, for example, that led to
Jefferson's statute of religious freedom. Today I may be the victim—
but tomorrow it may be you—until the whole fabric of our harmonious society is ripped apart at a time of great national peril.[37]

Some have suggested that the Houston meeting was the
turning point of the campaign as far as the religious issue was
concerned. The studied opinion of one correspondent who
was traveling with the campaign party was that Kennedy had
brought about little change in the opinions of the Houston
ministers or in Texas at large, but that his remarks might help
him in some other parts of the country.[38] More significant, however, for the purpose of an analysis of interfaith relations than
the immediate content of Kennedy's remarks is the fact that
the remarks were made before an explicitly church-related
gathering. This in itself indicated the growing awareness of
political America that even where politics were concerned the
ultimate changes in interfaith attitudes would have to come
through the churches themselves. It was no longer sufficient to
talk about the churches and their attitudes; it was now deemed
necessary to talk to the churches about interfaith concerns.
Even the body politic was acknowledging that the roots of improvement in Protestant-Catholic relationships were ecclesiastical ones.

To be sure, a great deal of anti-Catholic sentiment was
expressed during the 1960 campaign. Resolutions expressing
reservations about or opposition to a Catholic in the White
House were passed by several groups, some before the nominat-
ing conventions. Most of them, however, were smaller, ultraconservative, or fundamentalist bodies that were not in the
mainstream of recent Protestant thought.[39] Consequently, they
did not reflect any general Protestant sentiment. More significant than the passage of these resolutions were Protestant

statements released in opposition to the raising of the religious issue. Statements of this kind would have been unheard of a decade earlier. Their presence in 1960 was just further evidence of the changing interfaith climate in the country.

One of the best examples of this changing Protestant sentiment is the reaction of some well-known Protestant leaders to a statement made by a group known as the National Conference of Citizens for Religious Freedom, who claimed among their spokesmen Norman Vincent Peale, popular religious author and minister of the Marble Collegiate Church in New York City. The statement reviewed issues such as the Vatican envoy and parochial schools and concluded that the " 'religious' issue in the present political campaign . . . is created by the nature of the Roman Catholic Church which is, in a very real sense, both a church and also a temporal state."[40] Instead of unifying Protestant sentiment behind those views the statement was quickly countered from within Protestant circles. The *Christian Century* forthrightly denounced the statement and Reinhold Niebuhr and John C. Bennett, dean of Union Theological Seminary in New York, immediately issued a counterstatement declaring: "It is imperative that all voters realize that the persons who are raising the religious issue in this Presidential campaign certainly do not represent American Protestantism as a whole." [41]

As churchmen, Niebuhr and Bennett were giving evidence of a new sense of responsibility for constructive interfaith relations growing among American Protestants. For the first time in the nation's religious history anti-Catholicism was being put on the defensive by Protestants themselves. Reaction, in fact, was so strong to the statement of the National Conference of Citizens for Religious Freedom that Peale disassociated himself from the group,[42] and another of its better-known members, David Poling, a Protestant journalist, later modified his own stand.[43]

Further evidence of a new American Protestant orientation came when prominent bodies such as the American Lutheran Church, the Methodist General Conference, the General Assembly of the Southern Presbyterian Church, and the Council for Christian Social Action of the United Church of Christ all passed resolutions in their respective conventions before Kennedy's nomination denouncing the use of religion as an issue.[44] When anti-Catholic literature appeared during the Democratic primary campaign, thirteen well-known Protestant clergymen, including Edwin T. Dahlberg, president of the National Council of Churches, wrote an open letter to "fellow pastors in Christ" denouncing the literature, a letter which Kennedy himself gratefully acknowledged.[45] During the last month of the presidential campaign another series of Protestant protests against the religious issue occurred, climaxing in a strong reaction among Protestants to an effort on the part of some conservative and fundamentalist ministers to turn Reformation Sunday into an anti-Kennedy "Religious Liberty Sunday." As a result of the protests much less anti-Catholic preaching occurred on Reformation Sunday than had previously been anticipated.[46]

Other than resolutions, the anti-Catholicism during the campaign largely took the form of printed literature, especially tracts and pamphlets. Scurrilous literature had appeared as early as the Wisconsin primary in April,[47] but it tended to increase during the fall, when the anti-Catholic resolutions were subsiding, and it got much heavier during the last month of the campaign. A little over two months before election day, the Fair Campaign Practices Committee expressed fear that the literature might exceed that of 1928.[48] The Justice Department found 144 producers of this literature during the campaign, most of them with ultraconservative Protestant connections and undivulged financial backers.[49]

Efforts at evaluating the strength of the religious issue vary widely in their conclusions. Sorenson in his book *Kennedy* concludes that religion was "the largest factor in the campaign."[50] James Wine of the Kennedy organization remarks that the religious issue was more extensive "by a considerable margin" than in 1928.[51] Less than three weeks before election day, though, both Kennedy and his Republican opponent

Richard Nixon stated that religion was less of an issue than it had been when Al Smith had run.[52]

Whatever may be said about the effect of Kennedy's religion on the vote, the one clear fact is that his Catholicism did not keep him from winning. In spite of the closeness of the election, Kennedy's popular vote of 34,117,000 more than doubled the 15,016,000 that Al Smith had received and considerably exceeded the increase in Catholic voters between those two elections.[53] This in itself demonstrates a strong shift in Protestant attitudes within the country. As Sorenson remarks—even after his discussion of the magnitude of the religious issue—"John Kennedy could not have been elected President without the votes he received from Protestants as well as Catholics and Jews—indeed, more Protestants voted for him than all his Catholic and Jewish supporters combined."[54]

Especially remarkable is the fact that the election of a Roman Catholic to the presidency came less than a decade after the nation had been embroiled in the bitter conflicts between Protestants and Catholics which had raged through the 1940s and into the early 1950s. It is extremely doubtful that Kennedy could have been elected in 1956 had every other circumstance but the religious outlook of the nation been the same. In 1952 it would have been out of the question. And when one compares the milieu of interfaith dynamics of 1960 with that of 1939, the altered interfaith patterns in the country became even more evident. The year 1939 had been preceded by over a decade of organized nationwide emphasis on brotherhood and good will among those of differing religious affiliations, and yet when a representative of the president appeared in Rome, an open conflict arose almost overnight. The year 1960 was less than a decade away from one of the stormiest periods in all of America's interfaith history, and yet when a Catholic ran for the office of president itself, he was elected in spite of efforts by some religious groups to keep him out.

The changes in interfaith patterns during the late 1950s, therefore, took place at a much deeper and more influential level than had those of the 1930s. When one reviews the kinds of efforts at improving attitudes which took place during the five years before the 1960 election, one is struck by their definitely ecclesiastical and theological nature. Not one organized and publicized national effort at improvement of Protestant-Catholic political relations had occurred during those five years or for that matter during the entire decade of the 1950s. Neither was there any economic factor of the magnitude of the Depression to make cooperation a must for survival. Nor had there been a major war to make cooperation necessary for the nation's security since the days of Korea, which had actually been days of heated Catholic-Protestant arguments in America. Instead, there were books such as George Tavard's *Catholic Approach to Protestantism*, Jaroslav Pelikan's *Riddle of Roman Catholicism*, and Robert McAfee Brown and Gustave Weigel's *American Dialogue*. There were dialogues in religious publications such as the June 19, 1959, issue of *Christianity and Crisis*, and projects such as the Lutheran Institute for Roman Catholic theology studies in Minneapolis. The election of Kennedy occurred not during a period of major emphasis on interfaith improvement in the political arena, as the large amount of anti-Catholic sentiment against JFK during the campaign showed, but in the midst of an actual religious reorientation in America. It is especially significant that the strongest non-Catholic voices against the existence of the religious issue came from Protestant bodies in convention and from men who were in seminaries, on national church councils, in religious journalism, or in influential pulpits—men like Reinhold Niebuhr, John C. Bennett, Edwin T. Dahlberg, and G. Elson Ruff.[55] And it seems likely that the combined influence of all these sources could have easily swayed Protestants numbering eight thousand, Kennedy's majority in the popular vote.

Also significant is the change in American Catholic attitudes during the campaign. Given the magnitude of the situation, there was an amazingly small amount of ecclesiastical self-defense by the Catholic establishment. This was reflected even in the difference in Kennedy's campaign style from that of Al Smith. Once the religious issue was forced upon him, Smith had taken pains to explain things about his church and to show it in harmony with American precepts. Kennedy, however, simply concentrated on his public record and let the religious issue answer to that.[56] Furthermore, he came out solidly against both a Vatican embassy and federal aid to parochial schools. The styles in part reflect each man's personality, but this is only part of the story. The change in emphasis also showed a definite change in the status of the Catholic church in the country. In 1928 Catholicism was still in a secondary role in America, and its rapid growth was creating adjustment problems for the Protestant majority. This forced Catholicism, not yet secure, to expound its virtues for the sake of being better accepted. But in 1960 Catholicism in America was secure enough to feel no need of defense. The Catholic Church had been "of age" in America for several years now and so it was a matter not of proving its worth but of waiting for the nation to make a full adjustment to its maturity.

From within the inner circles of the church there was even some playing down of the prospect of a Catholic in the White House. Some went so far as to say that a Catholic who would vote for a candidate simply because the latter was also a Catholic would be sinning.[57] Cardinal Spellman himself did not divulge his preference of candidates even to his closest associates. The Vatican was neutral.[58] Catholic leaders who spoke to the religious question tended to do so largely in reaction to specific occurrences, such as John Courtney Murray's response to Norman Vincent Peale's group,[59] or by stressing, as did William Cardinal McIntyre of Los Angeles, not the safety of the Catholic church but the idea that religion should simply not be an issue at all.[60] Generally, the Catholic response to the whole question was that of a body which knew it was established in American religious life and felt no necessity of pushing its advantage, even if the result might be the election of one of its own as president of the country.

Just before the inauguration of Kennedy, Protestant evangelist Billy Graham held a joint news conference with the president-elect and stated that the election of a Catholic demonstrated that there was less religious prejudice in the country than many had supposed.[61] It was to the credit of both Protestants and Catholics that the religious tensions had, in fact, lessened considerably during the previous five to ten years. And so the election of Kennedy must be seen not as the beginning of a new era in American interfaith relations but as the reflection of a new era already in progress.

What the Kennedy years did do was to serve as a catalyst for the new era's development. The new president stood forthrightly for federal aid to public education and equally firm against federal aid to parochial schools. In this stand he was opposed by some of his fellow Catholics and praised by numbers of Protestants. Sorenson quotes Kennedy as quipping that the new debates over federal aid had "new teams."[62] Now, some Protestants who had opposed him during the campaign found themselves regarding Kennedy with new favor. The 1961 Southern Baptist Convention, for example, sent the president a telegram thanking him for his stand on the federal aid question.[63] Though there was debate on the bill, the religious issue of a Catholic in the White House greatly diminished. By late 1962 Protestant fears about a Catholic in the White House had been generally calmed. One of the Houston Protestant ministers before whom Kennedy had appeared during the campaign stated that "The religious issue has just paled away."[64] The federal aid debates, though resulting in another stalemate, never reached the crisis stage of the late 1940s and this in itself was notable evidence of the new interfaith patterns. Ameliorating voices from both groups further reflected the new maturity of relationships which had been developing since the mid-1950s. Cardinal Cushing of Boston admonished Catholics not to block all federal aid just because they "do not get their own way" concerning provisions for parochial schools.[65] The Protestant *Christianity and Crisis* showed a definite movement in the early 1960s further and further away from a typically Protestant stand of opposition to all forms of federal aid to parochial education and less than a month before the assassination of the president urged "Protestants, Catholics, Jews, and secularists to pay less attention to rigid traditions . . . and more attention to the needs of our children and youth."[66]

Once again, though, it was not American politics which would bring on the most vital changes in the patterns of Protestant-Catholic relations. Rather, it was, as had been the case since the mid-1950s, in the ecclesiastical context that the biggest advances were made. And involving, as it did, a non-American source the growth in improved relationships showed once more that leadership in changing interfaith patterns lay ultimately within the religious communities themselves, not in national political events or national civic-sponsored programs.

The beginnings of this most significant catalyst in improved worldwide and consequently in improved American interfaith outlooks came in January 1959. On the twenty-fifth day of that month Pope John XXIII, who had been in office less than three months, surprised the whole Christian world by calling an ecumenical council. There had been no prior indication that the Pope had such a momentous decision in mind. There had been no public conferences leading up to the announcement. Those who in subsequent months investigated the background of the decision could find only one occasion on which the Pope had mentioned the possibility of a council before he made the announcement. This was a private talk with his secretary of state, Cardinal Tardini, late in 1958 in which the two men had what one writer termed "a troubled conversation regarding the state of the world and the Church's role in it."[67] According to reports, during the conversation Pope John suddenly exclaimed, "A Council!"[68] Cardinal Tardini immediately approved, although he told the people in the Curia that the Pope would soon forget the idea.[69]

However, the Pope did not forget. The idea was confirmed in his mind in January 1959, during the Church Unity Octave, eight days which many Christian bodies set aside each year for prayer for worldwide Christian unity.[70] His announcement came the week following the Octave. The text of the official Vatican communique was brief. It contained few details and set no date for the convening of the council.[71] Yet it still drew much attention. Some Catholics reportedly wondered if the Pope were serious.[72] American Catholics, though, generally assumed that he was and a writer in the Jesuit publication *America* suggested that "The Council, among its many incidental effects, may further a new approach by Catholics in this country toward the problem of interdenominational relations."[73]

Protestant reactions to the announcement reflected a variety of attitudes. Some, in various parts of the world, could not help but wonder why the Pope had chosen the word ecumenical to describe the council, since it had been used primarily by Protestants rather than by Catholics.[74] Protestant leaders in America were generally cautious. Though interfaith attitudes had improved considerably since the middle of the decade, still, in 1959, religious leaders hesitated to be too optimistic too quickly about overtures of good will. Many of them could remember well the disappointing decline of the brotherhood emphasis of the 1930s. Protestant writer Franklin Littell stated that "unless a miracle occurs" the council would simply be a "denominational synod."[75]

A few months after the Pope's announcement, as plans for the council were getting underway, public talk of the announcement subsided. Other events began to alter further the already changing interfaith patterns. It was an interesting twist of fate that the advent of John Kennedy came almost on the heels of the Pope's announcement. Those Protestants who knew of the plans for a council could not help but think about them occasionally. What effect it had on their voting attitudes during the presidential campaign is not known, but it is highly probable that it had some. What is certain is that the Kennedy years made many American Protestants more receptive to the council once it began. America's first Roman Catholic president had stuck to his promise of opposing federal aid to parochial schools and to his promise of not recreating any post at the Vatican and had convinced many doubtful Protestants that a Catholic could be trusted.

But even more influential in the long run were the theologically oriented dialogues that were occurring with more and more frequency during the years 1960–1962. This pattern had carried over from the half-decade previous to 1960, making the foundation of these dialogues predate both the Kennedy years and the announcement about the council. It was in less-publicized ecclesiastical roots, therefore, more than in the nationally observed political events that the real work of interfaith concern was carried on. Especially significant were the numerous local discussion groups based on "Rules for the Dialogue" which had appeared in Brown's and Weigel's book and which were later presented simultaneously by the *Christian Century* and the *Commonweal*.[76]

Furthermore, the Pope himself had occasional audience with American Protestant leaders. Brooks Hays, a former congressman and later a special adviser to President Kennedy, and a past-president of the Southern Baptist Convention, related with deep feeling at an ecumenical gathering in 1969 his own audience with Pope John when the latter said to the former, "We *are* brothers in Christ."[77] This audience was a remarkable event for leaders from two traditions often considered at opposite ends of the religious spectrum, and it was equally remarkable in that Hays, though a man of the political world and not a minister, both presented himself and was received as first of all a man of the church. Events like this reflected more and more the irenic nature of the developing Protestant-Catholic patterns.

When October 1962, the date for the convening of Vatican II, rolled around, Protestants in America showed a new, keen interest in the council. Some even packed their bags and headed for Rome as observers. Others spoke of a new hope for an affirmative religious response by all groups to the needs of the day. In this vein Roger Shinn of Union Theological Seminary in New York wrote, "If the council speaks with such a spirit, we will listen."[78] As Vatican II itself got underway, both Protestants and Catholics who followed the proceedings became quite conscious of the council's efforts to open itself to insights from all expressions of Christianity. Even though little other than preliminary organization occurred during the opening session[79] a new spirit of ecumenicity was definitely in the air, prodding the *Christian Century* to comment at the end of the first session: "While only the first session of the Second Vatican Council has been completed it is already evident that the council may prove to be the most important religious event of our time."[80]

The subsequent story of Vatican II bore out much of the *Christian Century*'s estimation. Three more sessions from 1963 through the council's conclusion in December 1965 brought before the whole religious world considerations ranging from liturgical reforms to the idea of decentralized authority to the theology of ecumenism to the question of religious liberty.[81] Protestants were not always happy with what they felt was too great a hesitancy on the part of Rome to adopt specific decrees on some of these topics, but they were quick to admit that changes were taking place which would be momentous in terms of interfaith attitudes for Catholics and consequently for Protestants themselves.[82]

The total impact of these changes was so great that it simply could not be measured. One historian of twentieth-century America said in private conversation that the study of Protestant-Catholic relationships had become like "tracing the streams to the ocean."[83] As early as 1964 a Lutheran research team which tried to determine the extent of Protestant-Catholic rapprochement declared that available material for the study was "virtually inexhaustible."[84] A progress report on Protestant-Catholic relations prepared in 1967 by some officials of the National Council of Churches stated in somewhat unsophisticated language: "Now we are trampling all over each other to be the first to proclaim acceptance of one another."[85]

The extent of the rapprochement may be seen in part by a quick look at the variety of contexts in which it occurred during the short period of the council and the years immediately following. One of the first was that of religious journalism. Although interfaith dialogue was definitely in existence by the time of Vatican II it became much more common in 1963, immediately after the close of the council's first session. With the first issue of *Commonweal* in that year, Robert McAfee Brown began a regular column called "A Protestant Viewpoint."[86] The first issue of the *Christian Century* for the same year, with a minimum of comment, changed its self-designation from "undenominational weekly" to "ecumenical weekly."[87] The following year the first issue of a new *Journal of Ecumenical Studies* appeared, with an editorial staff of both Catholics and Protestants.[88]

Another area affected was the academic community. One of the first of what was to be a growing number of Protestant-Catholic colloquiums took place at Harvard in March 1963, the significance of which was probably best summed up by the editors of the volume containing the papers read at the meeting. They said: "Ten years ago the Colloquium would have been an impossibility."[89] Soon the pattern moved to something more permanent than colloquiums. In December 1963 Yale announced the appointment of Stephan G. Kuttner, a Roman Catholic Church historian, to an endowed chair of Roman Catholic studies in the university's Department of Religious Studies.[90] By October 1964 Brown, Harvard, Stanford, Temple, and Western Michigan, as well as Yale, had Roman Catholics on their faculties in Religion, and Protestants were lecturing regularly in Catholic schools, including two Protestant theologians in the Philosophy and Theology departments of Webster College in Missouri.[91] The whole movement in academic circles reached a new level of interfaith cooperation in 1966, beginning with the pooling of faculties, library resources, and credits by Fordham and Union Theological Seminary in New York in what the *New York Times* described as "the first contractual sharing of graduate resources in theology between a Protestant and a Catholic institution."[92]

Within the academic circles the publications of both Catholic and Protestant scholars in religion showed that the ecumenical undertakings were, indeed, having an impact. The works of the mid-1960s were definitely irenic in tone. They included books by Catholic authors such as John P. Dolan's *History of the Reformation: A Conciliatory Assessment of Opposite Views*,

which presented an impressively objective study, noticeable for
its lack of polemics,[93] and Killian McDonnell's *John Calvin:
The Church, and the Eucharist,* in which a Benedictine scholar,
who has in personal correspondence described his "own role as
mediating understanding to both Protestants and Catholics,"[94]
presented a sympathetic view of the Genevan reformer's Eucha-
ristic teachings.[95] From the pen of a Protestant scholar there
came Robert P. Scharlemann's *Thomas Aquinas and John
Gerhard,* which concluded that the great medieval scholastic
philosopher and the seventeenth-century Protestant thinker
were actually very close together in the content of their thought
and that knowledge of that fact could greatly enhance the current Protestant-Catholic discussions.[96] There was, in the same
year as Scharlemann's book, another book by Jaroslav Pelikan,
who had already advanced the Protestant-Catholic dialogues
with his *Riddle of Roman Catholicism.* Pelikan's book bore the
title *Obedient Rebels* and the interesting subtitle *Catholic Substance and Protestant Principle in Luther's Reformation* and
demonstrated a definite interfaith spirit by undertaking a unified study of what Pelikan called in the preface "two of the
deepest concerns of my thought and scholarship, the Reformation of the sixteenth century and the ecumenical movement of
the twentieth."[97] All of this scholarship, Catholic and Protestant alike, served to show a definite difference in the ecumenical
spirit of the 1960s from the brotherhood movement of the
1930s, when the writings of scholars of both groups had remained bitterly polemic in spite of the external emphases on
good will.

Evidence of a new interfaith spirit mounted as new moves
within American ecclesiastical structures appeared in many
places. By 1964 it was becoming more and more common for
Protestant gatherings to hear Catholic speakers. Late that year
a signal event occurred when the Archdiocese of Santa Fe
joined the New Mexico Council of Churches in a move which
marked the first time in American religious history that an
entire Roman Catholic diocese had ever joined an otherwise
all Protestant and Orthodox council.[98] In 1966 another mile-

stone was reached when the National Council of Churches named a Jesuit priest, David J. Bowman, to the position of assistant director of the National Council's Faith and Order Department, a move which National Council General Secretary R. H. Edwin Espy described as "another stone in the foundations of our common life which have been growing with astonishing speed in our time."[99]

At the grass-roots level there was a 256-page publication called *Living Room Dialogues,* which appeared in 1965 under the joint editorship of the Reverend William Greenspun, C.S.P., and the Reverend William A. Norgren of the National Council of Churches and the joint publication of both the Paulist Press and the National Council. The book was specifically designed as resource material for lay groups of Protestants and Catholics who wished to discuss together many issues related to the growing concern for Christian unity. Its appearance testified to the growing irenic interfaith spirit in America which was characterized "not by the polemics of the past but by a new spirit of sincere inquiry."[100] Among the suggestions contained in the volume were some suggestions for common worship—something far beyond what previous attempts at bringing about interfaith harmony had been able to achieve.

It was in the numerous examples of joint worship services that the existence of a new era in American Protestant-Catholic relations was best demonstrated. It will be remembered that the *Christian Century* had remarked in 1935 concerning the Williamstown Institute of Human Relations that for all its positive thrusts the essential ingredient of genuine progress in interfaith relations—common worship—was missing. But after Vatican II's impact there was a whole new feeling. A good example was the joint worship service with overflow attendance conducted on the first Sunday in Advent 1964 by Protestant Episcopal and Roman Catholic clergymen and laymen in Cambridge, Massachusetts, with the official sanction of Richard Cardinal Cushing and Episcopal Bishop Anson Phelps Stokes.[101] In March 1965 *Newsweek* reported that "joint religious services between U.S. Protestants and Catholics have increased rapidly and warmed the relations between estranged Christians."[102] About a year later *Time*, with a bit of exaggeration, asserted that "hardly a church exists that has not been preached to by a minister of another faith." In April 1966 *Life* stated: "There is . . . a new ecumenism of worship."[103]

Both religious communities acknowledged the impact of the council even if they could not measure it. Catholic theologian Bernard Lambert wrote in 1964 that Catholic people in America "will have to get accustomed to a new type of inter-Christian and inter-Church relations."[104] A prominent American Catholic historian, the Right Reverend John Tracy Ellis, commented in private correspondence in 1964 that "Catholics were generally discouraged by their bishops from entering upon . . . dialogue . . . until the days of Vatican II. Now it has become a more or less common practice."[105] A Protestant observer at the council, Albert C. Outler, spoke of the council's bringing on an "epiphany of love,"[106] and Protestant Robert McAfee Brown wrote in the *Catholic World* in March 1966 that "the Council has actually opened more doors than anyone realizes."[107]

Just why there was so much rapprochement so quickly is a subject of much interest. In part the rapprochement was not simply the result of the council, for the emphasis on better interfaith attitudes had been going on in America since the mid-1950s. Vatican II was not a beginning but a catalyst. What the council did do was to give an official sanction to the movement of the times. It gave Roman Catholics who felt a need for the blessings of their church on their activities a new sense of freedom. At the same time it gave Protestants who still wondered about the attitudes of those in the authority structures of Roman Catholicism a new sense of confidence in Catholic sincerity. Protestants, even from the most loosely structured traditions, often feel more limited in interfaith relations by statements of the Catholic hierarchy than do Catholics themselves. Consequently, Vatican II broke through the barriers in many Protestant minds and gave Protestants a new sense of liberty in their relations with Catholics.

Furthermore, Vatican II moved the whole issue of Protestant-

Catholic relations in America from a national to a worldwide context. This had the good effect of toning down the social and political tensions inherent in the religious pluralism of the nation. Now the pressure was not so much that of jockeying for social and political influence but that of keeping pace with the winds of change within the international interfaith climate. In a real sense, one distinction between America's brotherhood movement of the 1930s and the days of Vatican II was that the latter received a much wider scope of attention and therefore could exert the pressure of its influence more than the former had been able to do. Protestant and Catholic leaders in America knew that worldwide interfaith opinion would be formed concerning the health of their relations in the United States. And in an era in which world opinion was so vital in all areas, religious America was more prone to act positively on the influences of the world ecumenical council than she would have been at almost any other time. Many religious leaders in America viewed interfaith harmony and interfaith activity as a matter necessary for survival.

In a real sense the rapid growth of harmonious interfaith activity during the days of Vatican II and after showed that there were people in both Protestant and Catholic circles who wanted this activity. National Council officials in their June 1967 report on relationships with Roman Catholicism put it well by saying: "Like lovers prevented by class status and family prejudice from openly seeing each other, now suddenly we are courting with minimum stigma or obstacle."[108] Activity of such scope as has been described in previous paragraphs just does not spring up without some prior, if unconscious, desire for it. The conflicts of the 1940s and early 1950s arose partly from the guilt felt by both Catholics and Protestants over their inability to live in harmony; in order to allay this guilt, each community tried to establish the righteousness of its particular viewpoints. The new interfaith spirit of the 1960s, with the official blessings of the church, therefore, gave a sense of release to many religious people, who seized opportunities to express this release with all the enthusiasm of new converts.

As with new converts, too, the initial enthusiasm was destined to subside. By 1967 the Protestant-Catholic ecumenical spirit in America showed signs of leveling off. Participants were beginning to take stock of their activities. A report by the National Council of Churches' Office of Ecumenical Affairs, on council relationships with Catholicism, in November, 1967, stated: "One gets an impression that we are in a period of consolidation, rather than of major new advance. Like a python which has swallowed a large meal, we appear to be digesting food we have already tasted." [109] Robert McAfee Brown, in a book titled *The Ecumenical Revolution* which appeared in late 1969, speaks of this process of leveling off, interpreting it not as a demise of the ecumenical spirit but as a maturing of it.[110] The whole process had been a further stage in the maturing of Protestant-Catholic relations in America generally.

Of course not all of religious America was in the center of the new era of interfaith harmony. Bigots from both groups still shouted at one another. POAU, in spite of its occasional efforts to appear otherwise, still was essentially anti-Catholic in nature. On a local level numerous people still harbored old feelings of suspicion toward the other group. It would be misguided optimism to assume that as a result of Vatican II, American interfaith relations reached perfection.

Still, one is impressed by the fact that thoroughgoing anti-Catholicism and stringent anti-Protestantism were no longer the rule in public interfaith expression—as they had been scarcely a decade and a half before. Though these attitudes still existed, they were not encouraged by the mainstreams of either tradition. There was still a consciousness of theological differences, but the very acts of defining them and discussing them rather than ignoring them or bickering over them suggested a desire for deeper levels of interaction. This desire was evidence of a new maturity that gave each group the inner freedom to face its own attitudes and presuppositions without being as threatened as in the past and to accept the other religious community as making a definite and positive contribution to religion in America.

With this new maturity the emphasis went beyond good will and brotherhood alone to a concern for genuine understanding and, in the minds of some, unity. The whole interfaith emphasis had become what Everett Clinchy, who had served the National Conference of Christians and Jews well, called "a new ball-game. [111] The perilous times of the late 1960s demanded a more unified and explicit religious influence, which in turn made affirmative interfaith attitudes imperative. In earlier periods— even during the brotherhood movements—Protestants and Catholics had looked upon one another basically as strangers. After Vatican II, for the first time in American religious history, large numbers from each tradition began seeing each other more and more as brothers. This step would not solve all the interfaith problems of the future. But it was a step that would have a lasting influence.

Appendix A.

*Excerpts from Papal Documents
Concerning Non-Catholic
Christian Bodies*

These excerpts will show the fairly consistent attitude of Rome toward Protestantism until the period of Vatican II, at which time the reader can observe some change in emphasis.

Encyclical *Mortalium animos,* issued by
Pope Pius XI, January 6, 1928, in response to
an invitation to attend the Protestant-sponsored
First World Conference on Faith and Order
in Lausanne, Switzerland

. . . there are some who declare and freely admit that Protestantism, as they call it, has rejected inadvisedly certain dogmas and certain practices of external worship which are certainly consoling and useful, which, on the contrary the Roman Church has retained. And they soon add, to be sure, that she has corrupted primitive religious practice by adding to it certain teaching which is at variance with the Gospel and which has been proposed to the faithful as of faith. They cite among these, and in first place, the primacy of jurisdiction which has been attributed to Peter and to his successors in the See of Rome. Among these men there are some, although they are not numerous, who would grant either a certain primacy of honor, or of jurisdiction or power; but they hold, all the same, that it does not proceed from divine right but rather from a certain consent on the part of the faithful. Others go so far as to desire that their assemblies—which could be called motley—be presided over by the Pontiff himself. But if it is possible to find many of these non-Catholic loudly preaching fraternal union in Christ Jesus, you will certainly find none to whom it occurs to submit himself to and obey the teaching and governing authority of the Vicar of Jesus Christ. Nevertheless they claim that they are willing to treat with the Roman Church, but on an equal footing, as equals to an equal. But if they could do so, there does not seem to be any doubt that they would have the intention that the pact, when concluded, would not oblige them to renounce their opinions, which are the real cause why they still wander at a loss outside Christ's fold.

Since this is the case, it is clear that the Holy See cannot participate, under any conditions, in these gatherings, nor is it lawful for Catholics, under any conditions, to participate in or to assist these enterprises. If they were to go, they would be attributing authority to an erroneous form of the Christian religion, entirely alien to the one Church of Christ. . . .

The union of Christians cannot be fostered otherwise than by promoting the return of the dissident to the one true Church of Christ, which in the past they so unfortunately abandoned.

Encyclical *Lux veritatis*, released by Pope Pius XI,
December 25, 1931, on the 1100th anniversary
year of the Council of Ephesus

Let them remember, especially those who preside over the flock separated from Us, what was the faith professed by their forebears at Ephesus: the same which this supreme Chair of truth, in the past as in the present, keeps intact and strenuously defends. Let them remember that the unity of the true faith rests on that unique rock established by Christ, and that this unity can be preserved in full security only by the supreme authority of the successors of Blessed Peter (a).

A few years ago We spoke at greater length of this unity of the Catholic religion in Our encyclical letter *Mortalium animos* (a). It will be useful here briefly to recall this matter to mind, since the hypostatic union of Christ, solemnly defined at the Council of Ephesus, contains and offers an image of that unity with which our Redeemer wished to adorn his Mystical Body, that is, the Church, "one body" (b) "compacted and joined" (c). For if the personal unity of Christ constitutes the mysterious exemplar to which He Himself willed to see the close union of the Christian society conform, this certainly could never be the result of an unreal union of many warring elements, but only of a single hierarchy, a single supreme teaching authority, a single rule of belief, and one faith embraced by all Christians. No intelligent man can fail to see this.

Encyclical *Mystici Corporis Christi*, issued
by Pope Pius XII, June 29, 1943

For those who do not yet belong to the visible organism of the Catholic Church, you know well, Venerable Brothers, that from the beginning of Our Pontificate We have committed them to the divine protection and guidance, solemnly affirming that, following in the footsteps of the Good Shepherd, We have nothing so much at heart as that they may have life and have it more abundantly (a). This solemn assurance, after having implored the prayers of the entire Church, We wish to reiterate in this Encyclical Letter, in which We have celebrated the praise of the "great and glorious body of Christ" (b), inviting all men, and each one in particular, in a most loving manner to yield themselves freely and willingly to the interior movements of divine grace so as to liberate themselves from that state in which no man can be sure of his own eternal salvation (c). For even if they should find themselves turned towards the Mystical Body of the Redeemer by unconscious desire and aspiration, they would lack very many and very great supernatural helps which it is possible to enjoy only in the Catholic Church. Therefore, let them enter into Catholic unity, and joined with Us in the one organism of the Body of Jesus Christ, let all hasten to the one Head in a most glorious society of love (d). Without ever interrupting Our prayers to the Spirit of love and truth, We await them, with arms wide open, as those who approach, not a stranger's house, but the home of their father.

A Directive to the Bishops on Ecumenism issued by Pope Pius XII on December 20, 1949

In the same way they will take care that, under the false pretext that we should attend to what unites us rather than to what separates us, there be not fostered a dangerous indifferentism especially among those who are less well versed in theological matters and less profoundly anchored in their religion. For it is to be feared lest because of the so-called *irenical* spirit the Catholic doctrine—whether in questions of dogma or in questions of truths connected with dogma—by a comparative study or the vain desire of a kind of progressive assimilation of differing professions of faith, the Catholic doctrine itself be assimilated or in some way accommodated to the teaching of the dissidents, so that the purity of Catholic teaching would suffer, or its true and certain meaning in some way be obscured.

They will carefully avoid and firmly insist upon the fact that in teaching the history of the Reformation and the Reformers, the failings of Catholics not be exaggerated and the faults of the Reformers not be dissembled, or that the more accidental aspects of the question not be so highlighted that what is essential is hardly seen or felt; the defection from the Catholic faith.

Catholic doctrine must be propounded and explained in its *totality* and in its *integrity*; it is not permitted to pass over in silence or to veil in ambiguous terms what is comprised in the Catholic truth on the true nature and stages of justification, on the constitution of the Church, on the primacy of jurisdiction of the Roman Pontiff, on the unique true union by the return of separated Christians to the one true Church of Christ. Certainly they can be taught that in returning to the Church they will lose nothing of the good which, by God's grace, they have accomplished up to the present, but rather that by this return it will be completed and rendered perfect. But this should not be said in such a way that it would seem to them that in returning to the Church they would be bringing something substantial to it, which, up to that moment, had been lacking. These things must be said clearly and unambiguously, first because they are seeking the truth, then because outside the truth no true union is possible.

A Degree On Ecumenism promulgated November 21, 1964, by Vatican Council II

Even in the beginnings of this one and only Church of God there arose certain rifts (cf. I Cor. 11, 18–19; Gal. 1, 6–9; I Jn. 2, 18–19), which the Apostle strongly condemned (cf. I Cor. 1, 11 sqq; 11, 22). But in subsequent centuries much more serious dissensions made their appearance and quite large communities came to be separated from full communion with the Catholic Church—for which, often enough, men of both sides were to blame. The children who are born into these Communities and who grow up believing in Christ cannot be accused of the sin involved in the separation, and the Catholic Church looks upon them as brothers. . . . For men who believe in Christ and have been truly baptized are in real communion with the Catholic Church even though this communion is imperfect. The differences that exist in varying degrees between them and the Catholic Church—whether in doctrine and sometimes in discipline, or concerning the structure of the Church—do indeed create many obstacles, sometimes serious ones, to full ecclesiastical communion. The ecumenical movement is striving to overcome these obstacles. But even in spite of them it remains true that all who have been justified by faith in baptism are members of Christ's body (cf. CONC. FLORENTINUM, Sess. VIII [1439], *Dectruem Exultate Deo: Mansi* 31, 1055 A), and have a right to be called Christian, and so are with solid reasons accepted as brothers by the children of the Catholic Church (cf. S. AUGUSTINUS, *In Ps.* 32, *Enarr.* II, 29: PL 36, 299). . . .

In certain special circumstances, such as the prescribed prayers "for unity," and during ecumenical gatherings, it is allowable, indeed desirable that Catholics should join in prayer with their separated brethren. Such prayers in common are certainly an effective means of obtaining the grace of unity, and they are a true expression of the ties which still bind Catholics to their separated brethren. "For where two or three are gathered together in my name, there am I in the midst of them" (Mt. 18, 20).

Yet worship in common (*communicatio in sacris*) is not to be considered as a means to be used indiscriminately for the restoration of Christian unity. There are two main principles governing the practice of such common worship: first, the bearing witness to the unity of the Church, and second, the sharing in the means of grace. . . .

It is the urgent wish of this holy council that the measures undertaken by the sons of the Catholic Church should in practice develop in step with those of our separated brethren. No obstacle must be placed to the ways of divine Providence or any limit set to the future inspirations of the Holy Spirit. The council moreover professes its awareness that human powers and capacities cannot achieve this holy objective—the reconciling of all Christians in the unity of the one and only Church of Christ. It is because of this that the council rests all its hope on the prayer of Christ for the Church, on our Father's love for us, and on the power of the Holy Spirit. "And hope does not disappoint, because God's love has been poured into our hearts through the Holy Spirit, who has been given to us" (Rom. 5, 5).

The Declaration on Religious Freedom, Promulgated December 7, 1965, by Vatican Council II

This Vatican Council declares that the human person has a right to religious freedom. This freedom means that all men are to be immune from coercion on the part of individuals or of social groups and of any human power, in such wise that no one is to be forced to act in a manner contrary to his own beliefs, whether privately or publicly, whether alone or in association with others, within due limits.

The council further declares that the right to religious freedom has its foundation in the very dignity of the human person as this dignity is known through the revealed word of God and by reason itself. This right of the human person to religious freedom is to be recognized in the constitutional law whereby society is governed and thus it is to become a civil right.

The freedom or immunity from coercion in matters religious which is the endowment of persons as individuals is also to be recognized as their right when they act in community. Religious communities are a requirement of the social nature both of man and of religion itself.

Provided the just demands of public order are observed, religious communities rightfully claim freedom in order that they may govern themselves according to their own norms, honor the Supreme Being in public worship, assist their members in the practice of the religious life, strengthen them by instruction, and promote institutions in which they may join together for the purpose of ordering their own lives in accordance with their religious principles.

Appendix B.

Excerpts from United States
Supreme Court Decisions
on Matters Related to
Parochial Schools

The reader can note the generally consistent tendency of the court to decide in favor of the parochial schools' positions.

> *Meyer* v. *Nebraska*, a 1923 decision striking down
> a Nebraska law which had prohibited the teaching
> of foreign language in public and private schools

The problem for our determination is whether the statute as construed and applied unreasonably infringes the liberty guaranteed to the plaintiff in error by the Fourteenth Amendment. "No State shall . . . deprive any person of life, liberty, or property, without due process of law."

While this Court has not attempted to define with exactness the liberty here guaranteed, the term has received much consideration and some of the included things have been definitely stated. Without doubt, it denotes not merely freedom from bodily restraint but also the right of the individual to contract, to engage in any of the common occupations of life, to acquire useful knowledge, to marry, establish a home and bring up children, to worship God according to the dictates of his own conscience, and generally to enjoy those privileges long recognized at common law as essential to the orderly pursuit of happiness by free men. . . . The established doctrine is that this liberty may not be interfered with, under the guise of protecting the public interest, by legislative action which is arbitrary or without reasonable relation to some purpose within the competency of the State to effect. Determination by the legislature of what constitutes proper exercise of police power is not final or conclusive but is subject to supervision by the courts. *Lawton* v. *Steele*, 152 U. S. 133, 137. . . .

The challenged statute forbids the teaching in school of any subject except in English; also the teaching of any other language until the pupil has attained and successfully passed the eighth grade, which is not usually accomplished before the age of twelve. The Supreme Court of the State has held that "the so-called ancient or dead languages" are not "within the spirit or the purpose of the act." . . .

That the State may do much, go very far, indeed, in order to improve the quality of its citizens, physically, mentally and morally, is clear; but the individual has certain fundamental rights which must be respected. The protection of the Constitution extends to all, to those who speak other languages as well as to those born with English on the tongue. Perhaps it would be highly advantageous if all had ready understanding of our ordinary speech, but this cannot be coerced by methods which conflict with the Constitution—a desirable end cannot be promoted by prohibited means. . . .

As the statute undertakes to interfere only with teaching which involves a modern language, leaving complete freedom as to other matters, there seems no adequate foundation for the suggestion that the purpose was to protect the child's health by limiting his mental activities. It is well known that proficiency in a foreign language seldom comes to one not instructed at an early age, and experience shows that this is not injurious to the health, morals or understanding of the ordinary child.

The judgment of the court below must be reversed and the cause remanded for further proceedings not inconsistent with this opinion.

Pierce v. *Society of Sisters,* a 1925 decision
ruling against an Oregon law which had outlawed
parochial elementary education

. . . the Fourteenth Amendment guaranteed appellees against the deprivation of their property without due process of law consequent upon the lawful interference by appellants with the free choice of patrons, present and prospective. It declared the right to conduct schools was property and that parents and guardians, as a part of their liberty, might direct the education of children by selecting reputable teachers and places. Also, that these schools were not unfit or harmful to the public, and that enforcement of the challenged statute would unlawfully deprive them of patronage and thereby destroy their owners' business and property. Finally, that the threats to enforce the Act would continue to cause irreparable injury; and the suits were not premature.

No question is raised concerning the power of the State reasonably to regulate all schools, to inspect, supervise and examine them, their teachers and pupils; to require that all children of proper age attend some school, that teachers shall be of good moral character and patriotic disposition, that certain studies plainly essential to good citizenship must be taught, and that nothing be taught which is manifestly inimical to the public welfare.

The inevitable practical result of enforcing the Act under consideration would be destruction of appellees' primary schools, and perhaps all other private primary schools for normal children within the State of Oregon. These parties are engaged in a kind of undertaking not inherently harmful, but long regarded as useful and meritorious. Certainly there is nothing in the present records to indicate that they have failed to discharge their obligations to patrons, students or the State. And there are no peculiar circumstances or present emergencies which demand extraordinary measures relative to primary education.

Under the doctrine of *Meyer* v. *Nebraska,* 262 U. S. 390, we think it entirely plain that the Act of 1922 unreasonably interferes with the liberty of parents and guardians to direct the upbringing and education of children under their control. As often heretofore pointed out, rights guaranteed by the Constitution may not be abridged by legislation which has no reasonable relation to some purpose within the competency of the State. The fundamental theory of liberty upon which all governments in this Union repose excludes any general power of the State to standardize its children by forcing them to accept instruction from public teachers only. The child is not the mere creature of the State; those who nurture him and direct his destiny have the right, coupled with the high duty, to recognize and prepare him for additional obligations.

Cochran v. *Board of Education,* a 1930 decision
upholding a Louisiana law providing free
textbooks to parochial school children

The operation and effect of the legislation in question were described by the Supreme Court of the State as follows (168 La., p. 1020):

"One may scan the acts in vain to ascertain where any money is appropriated for the purchase of school books for the use of any church, private, sectarian or even public school. The appropriations were made for the specific purpose of purchasing school books for the use of the school children of the state, free of cost to them. It was for their benefit and the resulting benefit to the state that the appropriations were made. Thus, these children attend some school, public or private, the latter, sectarian or non-sectarian, and that the books are to be furnished them for their use, free of cost, whichever they attend. The schools, however, are not the beneficiaries of these appropriations. They obtain nothing from them, nor are they relieved of a single obligation, because of them. The school children and the state alone are the beneficiaries. It is also true that the sectarian schools, which some of the children attend, instruct their pupils

in religion, and books are used for that purpose, but one may
search diligently the acts, though without result, in an effort
to find anything to the effect that it is the purpose of the state to
furnish religious books for the use of such children. . . . What
the statutes contemplate is that the same books that are furnished children attending public schools shall be furnished
children attending private schools. This is the only practical
way of interpreting and executing the statutes, and this is what
the state board of education is doing. Among these books, naturally, none is to be expected, adapted to religious instruction."

The Court also stated, although the point is not of importance in relation to the Federal question, that it was "only the
use of the books that is granted to the children, or, in other
words, the books are lent to them."

Viewing the statute as having the effect thus attributed to it,
we cannot doubt that the taxing power of the State is exerted
for a public purpose. The legislation does not segregate private
schools, or their pupils, as its beneficiaries or attempt to interfere with any matters of exclusively private concern. Its interest
is education, broadly; its method, comprehensive. Individual
interests are aided only as the common interest is safeguarded.

Everson v. *Board of Education,* a 1947 decision
upholding a New Jersey law providing free
transportation to children going
to parochial schools

The "establishment of religion" clause of the First Amendment means at least this: Neither a state nor the Federal Government can set up a church. Neither can pass laws which aid
one religion, aid all religions, or prefer one religion over another. Neither can force nor influence a person to go to or to
remain away from church against his will or force him to pro-
fess a belief or disbelief in any religion. No person can be pun-
ished for entertaining or professing religious beliefs or
disbeliefs, for church attendance or non-attendance. No tax in

any amount, large or small, can be levied to support any religious activities or institutions, whatever they may be called, or whatever form they may adopt to teach or practice religion. Neither a state nor the Federal Government can, openly or secretly, participate in the affairs of any religious organizations or groups and *vice-versa*. In the words of Jefferson, the clause against establishment of religion by law was indeed to erect "a wall of separation between church and State." *Reynolds* v. *United States, supra* at 164.

We must consider the New Jersey statute in accordance with the foregoing limitations imposed by the First Amendment. But we must not strike that state statute down if it is within the State's constitutional power even though it approaches the verge of that power. See *Interstate Ry.* v. *Massachusetts,* Holmes, J., *supra* at 85,88. New Jersey cannot consistently with the "establishment of religion" clause of the First Amendment contribute tax-raised funds to the support of an institution which teaches the tenets and faith of any church. On the other hand, other language of the amendment commands that New Jersey cannot hamper its citizens in the free exercise of their own religion. Consequently, it cannot exclude individual Catholics, Lutherans, Mohammedans, Baptists, Jews, Methodists, Non-believers, Presbyterians, or the members of any other faith, *because of their faith, or lack of it,* from receiving the benefits of public welfare legislation. While we do not mean to intimate that a state could not provide transportation only to children attending public schools, we must be careful, in protecting the citizens of New Jersey against state-established churches, to be sure that we do not inadvertently prohibit New Jersey from extending its general state law benefits to all its citizens without regard to their religious belief. . . .

That Amendment (First Amendment) requires the state to be a neutral in its relations with groups of religious believers and non-believers; it does not require the state to be their adversary. State power is no more to be used so as to handicap religions than it is to favor them.

This Court has said that parents may, in the discharge of

their duty under state compulsory education laws, send their children to a religious rather than a public school if the school meets the secular educational requirements which the state has power to impose. See *Pierce* v. *Society of Sisters*, 268 U. S. 510. It appears that these parochial schools meet New Jersey's requirements. The State contributes no money to the schools. It does not support them. Its legislation, as applied, does no more than provide a general program to help parents get their children, regardless of their religion, safely and expeditiously to and from accredited schools.

The First Amendment has erected a wall between church and state. That wall must be kept high and impregnable. We could not approve the slightest breach. New Jersey has not breached it here.

Notes

I. Protestant Adjustment to Catholic Growth

1. Among the many sources dealing with the name-calling in the 1928 campaign is Edmund A. Moore, *A Catholic Runs for President: The Campaign of 1928* (New York: Ronald Press, 1956).

2. U.S., Department of Commerce, Bureau of the Census, *Historical Statistics of the United States: Colonial Times to 1957* (Washington, D.C., 1960), pp. 229–30.

3. See Gerald Shaughnessy, *Has the Immigrant Kept the Faith? A Study of Immigration and Catholic Growth in the United States, 1790–1920* (New York: Macmillan, 1925), pp. 145–82, for a generally contemporary study of those statistics.

4. John Tracy Ellis, *American Catholicism* (Chicago: University of Chicago Press, 1956), p. 122.

5. Interview with Canon Michael Hamilton of Washington National Cathedral, Washington, D. C., Nov. 18, 1969. For a study of urban influences on interfaith patterns in a particular time and place, see Kenneth Underwood, *Protestant and Catholic: Religious and Social Interaction in an Industrial Community* (Boston: Beacon Press, 1957).

6. An examination of the statistics for total population and for the various religious affiliations during the years leading up to and immediately following World War I can bear this out.

7. John Higham, *Strangers in the Land: Patterns of American Nativism, 1860–1925* (New Brunswick, N. J.: Rutgers University Press, 1955), p. 159.

8. For a treatment of immigration patterns during this period and some resulting issues, see George M. Stephenson, *A History of American Immigration, 1820–1924* (New York: Russell and Russell, 1964). Two acts were passed by Congress in the early 1920s limiting immigration, one in 1921 sponsored by Senator William P. Dillingham of Vermont, the other in 1924 sponsored by Congressman Albert Johnson of Washington. The earlier bill is listed by American Catholic historian John Tracy Ellis as a calendar event in the story of Catholicism in the United States. See Ellis, *American Catholicism*, p. 186.

9. Ellis, *American Catholicism*, p. 137.

10. See Everett R. Clinchy, *All in the Name of God* (New York: John Day, 1934), p. 138.

11. Higham, *Strangers in the Land*, and Gustave Myers, *History of Bigotry in the United States* (New York: Random House, 1943), both devote attention to an analysis of nativist attitudes.

12. Higham, *Strangers in the Land*, pp. 286ff.

13. Myers, *History of Bigotry*, p. 296.

14. P. 293.

15. A contemporary study of the Klan and its methods can be found in John Moffatt Mecklin, *The Ku Klux Klan: A Study of the American Mind* (New York: Harcourt, Brace, 1924). A more recent study is that of David M. Chalmers, *Hooded Americanism: The First Century of the Ku Klux Klan, 1865–1965* (Garden City, N. Y.: Doubleday, 1965).

16. Evans, "The Klan: Defender of Americanism," *Forum* 74 (Dec. 1925): 811.

17. *Ibid.*

18. Lowell Mellett, "Klan and Church," *Atlantic Monthly* 133 (Nov. 1923):588.

19. Higham, *Strangers in the Land*, p. 292.

20. Arnold S. Rice, *The Ku Klux Klan in American Politics* (Washington, D.C.: Public Affairs Press, 1962), p. 46.

21. *Literary Digest* 74 (Aug. 5, 1922):14.

22. See Oscar Handlin, *Al Smith and His America* (Boston: Little, Brown, 1958), pp. 118–23, and Emily Smith Warner, *The Happy Warrior: A Biography of My Father, Alfred E. Smith* (Garden City, N.Y.: Doubleday, 1956), pp. 149–64.

23. Higham, *Strangers in the Land*, p. 293.

24. John W. Owens, "Does the Senate Fear the K.K.K.?" *New Republic* 37 (Dec. 26, 1923):113–14. Rice, *The Ku Klux Klan*, p. 13, puts the membership in Indiana at 500,000.

25. Rice, *The Ku Klux Klan*, p. 13.

26. Reuben Maury, *The Wars of the Godly* (New York: Robert M. McBride, 1928), p. 283.

27. Myers, *History of Bigotry*, pp. 292–93.

28. Maury, *The Wars of the Godly*, pp. 283–84.

29. Mecklin, *The Ku Klux Klan*, p. 160.

30. Myers, *History of Bigotry*, pp. 287ff.

31. Maury, *The Wars of the Godly*, p. 289.

32. As quoted in "Protestants Disowning the Ku Klux," *Literary Digest* 75 (Nov. 25, 1922):23.

33. "Ku Klux Klan Condemned by the Religious Press," *Literary Digest* 71 (Oct. 1, 1921):30.

34. 118 (Dec. 1923):406–8.

35. Mellett, "Klan and Church," p. 589.

36. As quoted in Moore, *A Catholic Runs for President*, pp. 47–48.

37. *Ibid.*

38. Charles C. Marshall, "An Open Letter to Governor Smith," *Atlantic Monthly* 139 (April 1927):544.

39. Letters from Ellery Sedgwick, Jr., to author, June 24, 1970, and from Mrs. Marjorie Sedgwick to author, June 26, 1970.

40. *Atlantic Monthly* 139 (May 1927):721.

41. Correspondence from Miss Teresa FitzPatrick to author, July 16, 1970. This correspondence includes an article clipped from *Yankee*, Jan. 1968, containing recollections of Miss FitzPatrick's days with the *Atlantic*

Monthly, in which she mentions some of the episodes involving the Marshall-Smith correspondence. See Teresa FitzPatrick, "The Atlantic's Christine Lowell," *Yankee* (Jan. 1968):70–71, 126–33.

42. *Ibid.* The letter to author from Mrs. Marjorie Sedgwick also mentions the suit.

43. Alfred E. Smith, "Catholic and Patriot: Governor Smith replies," *Atlantic Monthly* 139 (May 1927):728.

44. Henry F. Pringle, *Alfred E. Smith: A Critical Study* (n.p.: Macy-Masiurs, 1927), p. 336.

45. *Ibid.* Moore, *A Catholic Runs for President*, pp. 77ff., makes similar observations about the impossibility of erasing the religious issue.

46. See Moore, *A Catholic Runs for President*, pp. 77–79.

47. See Myers, *History of Bigotry*, pp. 308–13, and Rice, *The Ku Klux Klan*, p. 89.

48. "The Week," *New Republic* 55 (July 11, 1928):181.

49. *Campaign Addresses of Governor Alfred E. Smith, Democratic Candidate for President, 1928* (Washington, D.C.: Democratic National Committee, 1929), pp. 25–26.

50. Moore, *A Catholic Runs for President*, pp. 121–25.

51. Warner, *The Happy Warrior*, p. 217.

52. From the Alfred E. Smith papers in the Museum of the City of New York.

53. *Campaign Addresses*, pp. 51–57.

54. *Campaign Addresses*. In Milwaukee on Sept. 29, Baltimore on Oct. 29, and New York City on Nov. 3, Smith made his strongest references, outside his Oklahoma City speech, to the religious issue.

55. Moore, *A Catholic Runs for President*, pp. 64, 110–28, 169.

56. *Ibid.*, p. 146.

57. *New York Times*, Sept. 29, 1928, pp. 1–2.

58. "The Whispering Campaign," *Christian Century* 45 (Sept. 20, 1928): 1120–21.

59. *New York Times*, Oct. 1, 1928, p. 3.

60. *Ibid.*, Nov. 9, 1928, p. 8.

61. Frank Graham, *Al Smith, American* (New York: G. P. Putnam's Sons, 1945), p. 206.

62. Letter from Everett R. Clinchy to author, June 24, 1970.

63. Quoted from the Dec. 24, 1920, Manifesto of the American Committee of the Rights of Religious Minorities, in James E. Pitt, *Adventures in Brotherhood* (New York: Farrar, Straus, 1955), p. 13.

64. Letter from Everett R. Clinchy to author.

65. *Ibid.*

66. John A. O'Brien, "They Fought against Ignorance with Spurs," reprint in pamphlet form from *Columbia Magazine* (April 1958):2.

67. Letter from Brown to author, July 7, 1970.

68. Letter from Clinchy to author. According to Sterling Brown in letter to author, the conference changed its name from "Jews and Christians" to "Christians and Jews" in 1939 because Jewish participants felt that an alphabetical designation was more appropriate, especially since Christians were a majority.

69. Will Herberg, *Protestant-Catholic-Jew: An Essay in American Religious Sociology* (Garden City, N.Y.: Doubleday, 1956), p. 266.

70. Letter from the Rev. E. V. Cardinal of St. Victor Rectory, Chicago, to author, July 27, 1964.

71. Herberg, *Protestant-Catholic-Jew*, p. 266.

72. 73 (March 1925):290–301.

73. Letter from Clinchy to author.

74. *Ibid.*

75. O'Brien, "They Fought against Ignorance," p. 2.

76. As quoted in Raymond Gram Swing, "Father Coughlin: The Wonder of Self-Discovery," *Nation* 139 (Dec. 26, 1934):731.

77. See *Father Coughlin's Radio Sermons, October 1930–April 1931, Complete* (Baltimore: Knox and O'Leary, 1931). Charles E. Coughlin, *Father Coughlin's Radio Discourses, 1931–1932* (Royal Oak, Mich.: The Radio League of the Little Flower, 1932). Charles E. Coughlin, *A Series of Lectures on Social Justice* (Royal Oak, Mich.: The Radio League of the Little Flower, 1935).

78. 13 (Jan. 28, 1931):343–45.

79. "Three Priests Preach the Gospel of Social Justice," *Literary Digest* 116 (Dec. 23, 1933):21.

80. As reported in *Newsweek* 5 (June 15, 1935):22.

81. Alice Roosevelt Longworth, "Strange Bedfellows," *Ladies' Home Journal* 52 (Oct. 1935):122.

82. Charles E. Coughlin, "A Third Party," *Vital Speeches of the Day* 2 (July 1, 1936):613–16. See also Charles J. Tull, *Father Coughlin and the New Deal* (Syracuse, N.Y.: Syracuse University Press, 1965).

83. See, for example, "Coughlin's Bullets," *Time* 28 (Oct. 5, 1936):33; "Coughlin Silenced," *Time* 30 (Oct. 18, 1937): 52; "Father Coughlin Gets a Taste of Discipline from His New Archbishop," *Newsweek* 10 (Oct. 18, 1937):37–38; and John A. Ryan, "Catholics and Anti-Semitism," *Current History* 49 (Feb. 1939):25–26.

84. *New York Times*, March 27, 1933, p. 10.

85. Oswald Garrison Villard, "Issues and Men: A Notable Conference," *Nation* 141 (Sept. 18, 1935):315.

86. *Ibid.*

87. *New York Times*, Sept. 3, 1939, p. 9. See also Pitt, *Adventures in Brotherhood*, p. 76.

88. Letter from Clinchy to author.

89. *New York Times*, April 7, 1934, p. 16.

90. *Ibid.*

91. *Ibid.*, Nov. 27, 1937, p. 8.

92. *Ibid.*, Feb. 13, 1938, II, p. 3.

93. Pitt, *Adventures in Brotherhood*, p. 68.

94. The *New York Times* reported several of these tours during the 1930s. A few of the periodical references to various ones of them include J. Elliott Ross, "An Ounce of Prevention," *Commonweal* 19 (Feb. 9, 1934):399–401; "Priest, Rabbi, and Dixie Hospitality," *Literary Digest* 119 (April 27, 1935):19; T. Lawrason Riggs, "A Good-Will Tour," *Commonweal* 21 (April 12, 1935):670; and "Tolerance: A Drive To Make America Safe for Differences," *Newsweek* 7 (June 6, 1936):28.

95. Mrs. Able J. Gregg, *New Relationships with Jews and Catholics* (New York: Association Press, 1934), p. 2.

96. "How Can Jews, Catholics, and Protestants Live Together?" *Christian Century* 51 (Nov. 28, 1934): 1508–9. See also "A New Williamstown Institute," *Commonweal* 22 (June 21, 1935):200.

97. Robert A. Ashworth, "Catholics Accept Mexican Program," *Christian Century* 52 (Sept. 11, 1935):1158. See also *Nation* 141 (Sept. 18, 1935):315.

98. *Christian Century* 52 (Sept. 11, 1935):1156.

99. *Ibid.*

100. "Religion and Human Relations," *Christian Century* 52 (Sept. 18, 1935):1166.

101. Carlton J. H. Hayes, "Significance of the Reformation in the Light of Contemporary Scholarship," *Catholic Historical Review* 17 (Jan. 1932): 399–400. This article was originally Hayes's presidential address to the American Catholic Historical Association meeting in Minneapolis in Dec. 1931.

102. John A. O'Brien, *The Faith of Millions: The Credentials of the Catholic Religion* (Huntington, Ind.: Our Sunday Visitor, 1938), p. 77.

103. "Calvin's Efforts toward the Consolidation of Protestantism," *Journal of Religion* 8 (July 1928):411–33.

104. "The Bible Rediscovered by the Protestant Reformers," *Union Seminary Review* 43 (Oct. 1931):25–34.

105. *New York Times*, Jan. 8, 1932, p. 13. See Appendix A for excerpts from the encyclical.

106. *Ibid.*, Dec. 26, 1935, through April 1936.

107. Letter from Clinchy to author.

II. *Catholicism in America Comes of Age*

1. *New York Times*, Jan. 3, 1939, p. 5.

2. *Ibid.*, April 14, 1939, p. 6, and May 21, 1939, p. 3.

3. The *Washington Post*, Dec. 24, 1939, pp. 1–2, reported that diplomatic circles in the capital considered the appointment as a step toward full diplomatic relations between the United States and the Vatican.

4. *New York Times*, Dec. 28, 1939, p. 1.

5. *Ibid.*, Jan. 10, 1940, p. 1.

6. *Ibid.*, Jan. 27, 1940, p. 4.

7. As reported by Religious News Service in "Churches Ask Taylor Recall," *Christian Century* 57 (May 1, 1940):487.

8. *New York Times*, Jan. 1, 1940, p. 8.

9. *Ibid.*, May 12, 1940, IV, p. 8.

10. "Interfaith Army: NCCJ Finds Anti-Semitism on the Wane, but Fears Taylor Row," *Newsweek* 15 (May 27, 1940):52.

11. "Cleveland Catholics Campaign for Control of Public Schools," *Christian Century* 58 (Nov. 19, 1941):1429–30.

12. "Religion Colors School Contest," *Christian Century* 58 (Nov. 19, 1941):1148.

13. U.S., Department of Commerce, Bureau of the Census, *Historical Statistics of the United States: Colonial Times to 1957* (Washington, D.C., 1960), p. 230.

14. See Harold Fey, "Can Catholicism Win America?" *Christian Century* 61 (Nov. 29, 1944):1378.

15. "Protestant Reorientation," *Christian Century* 60 (Oct. 27, 1943): 1222–24.

16. *Christian Century* 61 (Nov. 29, 1944):1378.

17. Harold Fey, "The Center of Catholic Power," *Christian Century* 62 (Jan. 17, 1945):76.

18. *New York Times*, Nov. 30, 1944, p. 36.

19. As reported in *ibid.*, Dec. 2, 1944, p. 11.

20. *Ibid.*, Oct. 29, 1945, p. 11.

21. *Ibid.*, April 17, 1945, p. 9.

22. *Ibid.*, Oct. 25, 1945, p. 13.

23. *Ibid.*, May 4, 1946, p. 8.

24. *Ibid.*, May 17, 1946, p. 4; May 27, 1946, p. 26; June 1, 1946, p. 11; June 6, 1946, p. 6.

25. *Ibid.*, June 6, 1946, p. 1.

26. *Ibid.*, June 12, 1946, p. 11, and June 14, 1946, pp. 1, 6.

27. *Ibid.*, Sept. 25, 1947, p. 4.

28. "Let the Senate Investigate the Taylor Embassy," *Christian Century* 64 (Oct. 14, 1947):1229.

29. *New York Times*, June 13, 1946, p. 1.

30. *Ibid.*, June 23, 1946, p. 12.

31. *Ibid.*, Dec. 9, 1946, p. 24.

32. *Ibid.*, April 15, 1950, p. 7.

33. Letter from General Mark W. Clark, U.S.A. (Ret.), to author, June 22, 1970.

34. *Ibid.*

35. *Ibid.*

36. *New York Times*, Oct. 21, 1951, p. 26.

37. *Ibid.*

38. *Ibid.*, p. 30.

39. *Ibid.*, Nov. 1, 1951, p. 17.

40. *Ibid.*

41. *Ibid.*, Nov. 29, 1951, p. 33. See also "Protesting Protestants," *Time* 58 (Dec. 10, 1951):77.

42. "Down the Road to Rome," *Nation* 173 (Nov. 3, 1951):368–70.

43. As reported in *New York Times*, Oct. 31, 1951, p. 15.

44. *Ibid.*, Jan. 14, 1952, p. 1.

45. Letter from General Mark Clark to author.

46. *Ibid.*

47. 262 U.S. 390–403 (1923). See also Anson Phelps Stokes, *Church and State in the United States* (New York: Harper and Brothers, 1950), 2:738, 741.

48. 268 U.S. 510–36 (1925). See also Vivian Trow Thayer, *Public Education and Its Critics* (New York: Macmillan, 1954), p. 43.

49. "Now Will Protestants Awake?" *Christian Century* 64 (Feb. 26, 1947): 262–63.

50. *New York Times*, May 8, 1947, p. 26.

51. "The Taft Education Bill, *Commonweal* 45 (March 14, 1947):532–33.

52. *New York Times,* Aug. 2, 1947, p. 14.

53. *North College Hill, Ohio: An Example of Some Effects of Board of Education Interference with Sound Administration of Public Education* (Report of an Investigation by the National Commission for the Defense of Democracy Through Education of the National Education Association of the United States, Nov. 1947). See also *New York Times,* July 11, 1947, p. 8, and Alson J. Smith, "The Catholic-Protestant Feud," *American Mercury* 65 (Nov. 1947):540–41.

54. Personal interview with William A. Cook, Feb. 1970.

55. Telephone conversation with Cook, Feb. 1970.

56. NEA Report on North College Hill.

57. *Ibid.,* p. 21.

58. *Ibid.*

59. See Library of Congress, *Digest of Public General Bills, 1947–48, 80th Cong., 1st sess.* (Washington, D.C., 1947), p. 29.

60. In *Commonweal* 45 (March 14, 1947):532–33, the Catholic journal notes this opposition. The *Commonweal* itself, however, supported the Taft bill, saying that its passage would not only be good for education but would also allay fears of Protestants over the New Jersey bus transportation decision.

61. For example, two large Southern-based groups, the Southern Baptist Convention and the Presbyterian Church in the U.S., openly opposed the Taft bill, the former in its annual meeting, the latter through its Christian Relations Committee. See *New York Times,* May 8, 1947, p. 22, and May 21, 1947, p. 4.

62. *New York Times,* April 2, 1948, p. 1. For House inaction on the Taft bill see Frank J. Munger and Richard F. Fenno, Jr., *National Politics and Federal Aid* (Syracuse, N.Y.: Syracuse University Press, 1962), p. 10. On the Aiken proposal see Zeno B. Katterle and Ruth E. Pike, *A Compilation of Laws and Proposals Relating to Federal Aid to Education* (Pullman, Wash.: State College of Washington, 1949), pp. 395–98.

63. *Federal Aid to Education: Hearings before Subcommittee No. 1 of the Committee on Education and Labor: House of Representatives: Eightieth Congress: First Session,* Vol. 1 (Washington, D.C., 1947), pp. 423–27, 458–575.

64. See Library of Congress, *Digest of Public General Bills, 1949–50, 81st Cong., 1st sess.* (Washington, D. C., 1949), p. 367.

65. *New York Times,* May 19, 1949, p. 34.

66. *Ibid.,* June 27, 1949, p. 20.

67. *Ibid.,* June 20, 1949, pp. 1, 20. For further comments on Spellman's position see Munger and Fenno, *National Politics,* p. 58.

68. See U.S., Congress, House, *Congressional Record,* 81st Cong., 2d sess., 1949, Appendix, vol. 95, pt. 16:5604.

69. Interview with Cook, Feb. 1970.

70. The complete text of the manifesto can be found in "Separation of Church and State: A Manifesto by 'Protestants and Other Americans United,'" *Christian Century* 65 (Jan. 21, 1948):79–82. See also Charles Clayton Morrison, "The Objectives of P.O.A.U.," *Christian Century* 66 (Feb. 23, 1949):236–39.

71. *Christian Century* 65 (Jan. 21, 1948):81–82.

72. Cook in personal interview with author.

73. 1 (May 15, 1948):1–3.

74. Joseph M. Dawson, *The Birth of POAU* (pamphlet) (Washington, D.C.: POAU, n.d.).

75. *New York Times*, Jan. 26, 1948, p. 17.

76. *Ibid.*, Jan. 13, 1948, p. 1.

77. *Ibid.*, Feb. 16, 1948, p. 5.

78. Letter from Blanshard to author.

79. Paul Blanshard, "The Catholic Church in Medicine," *Nation* 165 (Nov. 1, 1947):466–69; *idem*, "The Sexual Code of the Roman Church," *Nation* 165 (Nov. 8, 1947):496–99; *idem*, "The Catholic Church and Education," *Nation* 165 (Nov. 15, 1947):525–28.

80. Letter from Blanshard to author.

81. *Ibid.*

82. Harold C. Gardiner, "Analysis of a Smear Smut," *America* 78 (Dec. 6, 1947):267–68. The *Nation* reprinted this article in its Jan. 3, 1948, issue along with a reply by Blanshard and a counterreply by *America*'s editor, both of which had appeared in the Dec. 7, 1947, issue of *America*.

83. *New York Times*, Jan. 9, 1948, p. 23; Jan. 10, 1948, p. 17; Jan. 14, 1948, p. 28; Jan. 24, 1948, p. 17; and Jan. 28, 1948, p. 14. As noted in some of these news releases, a magazine called *Soviet Russia Today* was banned at the same time.

84. Letter from Blanshard to author.

85. See *Nation* 166 (April 10, 1948; May 1, 1948; May 8, 1948; May 15, 1948; May 22, 1948; May 29, 1948; and June 5, 1948). See also *New York Times*, June 24, 1948, pp. 1, 50.

86. *New York Times*, July and Aug. 1948.

87. (Boston: Beacon Press, 1949). The following book was written as a reply: James M. O'Neill, *Catholicism and American Freedom* (New York: Harper and Brothers, 1952).

88. Bryan M. O'Reilly, "Catholic America Comes of Age," *Catholic World* 166 (Jan. 1948):340–47.

89. Herberg, *Protestant-Catholic-Jew: An Essay in Religious Sociology* (Garden City, N.Y.: Doubleday, 1955), p. 251.

III. *Toward Relationships of Maturity*

1. J. B. Matthews, "Reds and Our Churches," *American Mercury* 77 (July 1953):3–13.

2. 58 (May 8, 1953):120.

3. "Protestant, Be Yourself!" *Christian Century* 72 (Oct. 19, 1955):1199.

4. John B. Sheerin, "Protestant-Catholic Cold War," *Catholic World* 182 (Dec. 1955):161–64.

5. "See P.O.A.U. as Ecumenical Body," *Christian Century* 73 (Feb. 8, 1956):190. On at least three occasions in 1955, letters to the *Christian Century* noted the lack of enthusiasm in the National Council for the work of POAU. See *Christian Century* 72 (Aug. 3, 1955):901; (Sept. 7, 1955):1057; and (Sept. 28, 1955):1117.

6. E.g., there were reports that at a national conference of POAU in 1957 the organization had referred to Vice President Nixon's once having hired a Catholic as a secretary as if this were a matter of serious concern. See "Father Murray and POAU," *America* 96 (Feb. 23, 1957):570.

7. *New York Times*, March 4, 1957, p. 46.

8. *Ibid.*

9. "A Lamentable 'Protestant' Strategy," *Christianity and Crisis* 17 (April 1, 1957):34.

10. "Other American Quits," *America* 98 (Feb. 15, 1958):555.

11. "Some Other Americans," *Commonweal* 69 (Dec. 26, 1958):328.

12. *New York Times*, Oct. 15, 1958, p. 3.

13. *America* 98 (Feb. 15, 1958):555.

14. Thurston N. Davis, "A Time for Silence or a Time to Speak," *America* 96 (March 16, 1957):670–72. See also *New York Times*, March 14, 1957, p. 59.

15. "Needed: Adult Discussion of Religion on Radio," *Christian Century* 74 (March 27, 1957):379.

16. Letter from Tavard to author, July 28, 1970.

17. *Ibid.*

18. George H. Tavard, *The Catholic Approach to Protestantism* (New York: Harper and Brothers, 1955).

19. H. A. Reinhold, "Revealing Example of Charity and Hope," *Commonweal* 63 (Dec. 16, 1955):288.

20. Harry M. Buck, "Over There," *Christian Century* 73 (Feb. 1, 1956):142.

21. Chicago: Regnery, 1955.

22. Will Herberg, *Protestant-Catholic-Jew: An Essay in American Religious Sociology* (Garden City, N.Y.: Doubleday, 1955), p. 7.

23. E.g., Gustave Weigel, "Americans Believe That Religion Is a Good Thing," *America* 94 (Nov. 5, 1955):150–54, and "Lonely Crowd at Prayer," *Christian Century* 73 (May 30, 1956):662–63.

24. R. L. Bond, "Belleville Promotes Understanding," *National Council Outlook* 7 (June 1957):5–6.

25. Malachi J. Donnelly, "Lutherans to Study Catholic Theology," *America* 97 (Aug. 31, 1957):536, and "Impossible Possibilities Foreshadowed," *Christian Century* 74 (Sept. 18, 1957):1091.

26. John B. Sheerin, "The Sin and Agony of Disunity," *Catholic World* 186 (Nov. 1957):82–85, and Gustave Weigel, "Faith and Order at Oberlin," *America* 98 (Oct. 19, 1957): 67–71.

27. 19 (June 8, 1959):87.

28. "We Talk Together," *America* 101 (June 27, 1959):467.

29. New York: Abingdon Press, 1959.

30. Letter from Brown to author, Aug. 31, 1969.

31. Robert McAfee Brown and Gustave Weigel, *An American Dialogue: A Protestant Looks at Catholicism and a Catholic Looks at Protestantism* (Garden City, N.Y.: Doubleday, Anchor Books, 1960).

32. *Ibid.*

33. On Kennedy as a vice-presidential hopeful see Charles A. H. Thomson and Frances M. Shattuck, *The 1956 Presidential Campaign* (Washington, D.C.: Brookings Institution, 1960), pp. 154–63.

34. *New York Times*, Aug. 25, 1960, p. 1.

35. Letter from Wine to author, July 22, 1970.

36. *Ibid.*

37. *New York Times*, Sept. 13, 1960, p. 22, carried the full transcript of Kennedy's speech plus the questions and answers.

38. *Ibid.*, Sept. 14, 1960, pp. 1, 32.

39. Examples included the American Baptist Association (not to be confused with the American Baptist Convention), the International Pentecostal Assemblies, the American Council of Christian Churches, and the National Association of Evangelicals. The last of these was the largest ultraconservative organization in America, though nowhere near the size of the mainstream Protestant body, the National Council of Churches. See *New York Times*, April 27, 1960, p. 16; April 30, 1960, p. 27; June 23, 1960, p. 12; and Aug. 5, 1960, p. 7.

40. *New York Times*, Sept. 8, 1960, p. 25.

41. *Ibid.*, Sept. 16, 1960, p. 18.

42. *Ibid.*

43. *Ibid.*, Oct. 17, 1960, p. 22.

44. *Ibid.*, Feb. 2, 1960, p. 23; April 21, 1960, p. 16; May 1, 1960, p. 57; and May 3, 1960, p. 1.

45. *Ibid.*, May 3, 1960, pp. 1, 28. Earlier, Dahlberg had issued a joint appeal with Roman Catholic and Jewish leaders for fairness during the campaign. See *ibid.*, Feb. 16, 1960, p. 4.

46. See *ibid.* for the month of Oct. and the first week of Nov. 1960. Note also "Reformation and Election," *Christian Century* 77 (Oct. 26, 1960): 1235–36.

47. *New York Times*, March 19, 1960, p. 10, and April 10, 1960, p. 50.

48. *Ibid.*, Aug. 25, 1960, p. 20.

49. *Ibid.*, Oct. 16, 1960, p. 56.

50. Theodore C. Sorenson, *Kennedy* (New York: Harper and Row, 1956), p. 217.

51. Letter from Wine to author.

52. *New York Times*, Oct. 20, 1960, p. 1.

53. Statistics on Catholic population in America from the Bureau of the Census and *The World Almanac* indicate that the total growth in numbers of Catholics in America, including all those below voting age, was in the neighborhood of 20 million. The 19 million difference in Kennedy's popular vote from that of Al Smith, therefore, would have to have included a substantial non-Catholic vote.

54. Sorenson, *Kennedy*, p. 223.

55. G. Elson Ruff was editor of the *Lutheran*, weekly publication of the United Lutheran Church in America.

56. Sorenson makes this observation in *Kennedy*, p. 109.

57. E.g., the *Catholic Review* of the archdiocese of Baltimore and the *Monitor* of the Trenton diocese. See *New York Times*, April 1, 1960, p. 39, and April 15, 1960, p. 11.

58. *New York Times*, Nov. 5, 1960, p. 9.

59. See "On Raising the Religious Issue," *America* 103 (Sept. 24, 1960): 702.

60. *New York Times*, June 24, 1960, p. 55.

61. *Ibid.*, Jan. 17, 1961, p. 24.

62. Sorenson, *Kennedy*, p. 357.

63. "Ecumenical Vibrations," *Time* 77 (June 2, 1961):63.

64. *New York Times*, Sept. 23, 1962, p. 10E.

65. *Ibid.*, Oct. 22, 1961, p. 58.

66. "Federal Aid to Education: A Call to Action," *Christianity and Crisis* 23 (Oct. 28, 1963):191.

67. Xavier Rynne, *Letters from Vatican City: Vatican Council II (First Session): Background and Debates* (New York: Farrar, Straus, 1963), p. 1.

68. *Ibid.* See also Robert Blair Kaiser, *Pope, Council, and World: The Story of Vatican II* (New York: Macmillan, 1963), p. 14, and George Cornell, *Voyage of Faith: The Catholic Church in Transition* (New York: Odyssey, 1966), pp. 32–33.

69. Kaiser, *Pope, Council, and World*, p. 14.

70. *Ibid.*, p. 15. See also Henri Daniel-Rops, *The Second Vatican Council: The Story behind the Ecumenical Council of Pope John XXIII* (New York: Hawthorne Books, 1962), p. 13.

71. *New York Times*, Jan. 26, 1959, p. 3.

72. Kaiser, *Pope, Council, and World*, pp. 16–17, says this was particularly true of French Catholics.

73. Robert A. Graham, "Will Christians Come Together?" *America* 100 (Feb. 28, 1959):628.

74. Kaiser, *Pope, Council, and World*, p. 18.

75. Franklin J. Littell, "The Pope's Ecumenical Council," *Christian Century* 76 (Feb. 25, 1959):225.

76. Brown and Weigel, *An American Dialogue*, pp. 26–34. And see Robert McAfee Brown, "Rules for the Dialogue," *Christian Century* 77 (Feb. 17, 1960):183–85, and *Commonweal* 71 (Feb. 19, 1960): 563–66. For two examples of references to dialogue see John B. Mannion, "The Layman and the Dialogue," *Catholic World* 193 (Aug. 1961):280–87, and Charles H. Bayer, "Dialogue in Suburbia," *Christian Century* 79 (March 28, 1962):399.

77. Remarks made at the Wake Forest Ecumenical Institute Conference of Roman Catholics and Southern Baptists, Wake Forest University, Winston-Salem, N. C., May 8–10, 1969.

78. Roger L. Shinn, "Hopes for the Second Vatican Council," *Christianity and Crisis* 22 (Oct. 1, 1962):159.

79. On the first session see Kaiser, *Pope, Council, and World*; George A. Lindbeck, ed., *Dialogue on the Way: Protestants Report from Rome on the Vatican Council* (Minneapolis: Augsburg Publishing House, 1965), pp. 18–46; and Rene Laurentine, "Vatican II: Report on the First Session," *Cross Currents* 13 (Fall 1963):401–76.

80. "Vatican without Walls," *Christian Century* 80 (Jan. 2, 1963):3.

81. There are numerous collections of Vatican II's proceedings. E.g., Xavier Rynne, *The Second Session: The Debates and Decrees of Vatican Council II, September 29 to December 4, 1963* (New York: Farrar, Straus, 1964), and *idem, The Third Session: The Debates and Decrees of Vatican Council II, September 14 to November 21, 1964* (New York: Farrar, Straus, and Giroux, 1965).

82. See such periodicals as the *Christian Century* and *Christianity and Crisis* for the years 1963–1965.

83. Maurice M. Vance, professor of history, Florida State University, in conversation with author, Summer 1967.

84. Cornell, *Voyage of Faith*, p. 224.

85. "Progress Report on the Relationship between the National Council of the Churches of Christ in the U.S.A. and Roman Catholicism" (unpublished report prepared for presentation to the General Board of the National Council of Churches, June 1–2, 1967), p. 2.

86. "Catholic Journalist, Protestant Columnist," *Commonweal* 77 (Jan. 4, 1963):388.

87. "Typographically Your Century," *Christian Century* 80 (Jan. 2, 1963):4.

88. See "The Purpose of the Journal of Ecumenical Studies," *Journal of Ecumenical Studies* 1 (Winter 1964):iii.

89. Samuel H. Miller and G. Ernest Wright, eds., *Ecumenical Dialogue at Harvard: The Roman Catholic-Protestant Colloquium* (Cambridge, Mass.: Belknap Press of Harvard University Press, 1964), p. vii.

90. *New York Times*, Dec. 16, 1963, p. 65.

91. "Reformation Sunday," *Commonweal* 81 (Oct. 30, 1964):150.

92. Feb. 20, 1966, pp. 1, 36.

93. New York: Deselee Company, 1965.

94. Letter from McDonnell to author, Sept. 3, 1969.

95. Princeton, N.J.: Princeton University Press, 1967.

96. New Haven: Yale University Press, 1964, p. 1.

97. New York: Harper and Row, 1964, preface.

98. "Ecumenical First," *Christian Century* 82 (Jan. 6, 1965):6–7.

99. *New York Times*, July 16, 1966, p. 11.

100. New York and Glen Rock, N.J.: National Council of the Churches of Christ in the U.S.A. and Paulist Press, 1965, p. 7.

101. "Hold Unprecedented Ecumenical Service," *Christian Century* 81 (Dec. 16, 1964):1548.

102. "Vatican Special Delivery," *Newsweek* 65 (March 15, 1965):64.

103. "The Ecumenical Spirit, Easter, 1966," *Life* 60 (April 8, 1966):4.

104. As quoted in Cornell, *Voyage of Faith*, p. 22.

105. Letter from Ellis to author, July 2, 1964.

106. "Council of New Beginnings," *America* 113 (Dec. 18–25, 1965): 771–72.

107. "Vatican II: What Does the Future Hold?" *Catholic World* 202 (March 1966):342.

108. Unpublished report on "National Council of Churches–Roman Catholic Relations," June 1967, p. 2.

109. "A Report on Relations between the Roman Catholic Church and the National Council of Churches of Christ in the U.S.A." (unpublished report prepared by the Office of Ecumenical Affairs of the National Council of Churches, Nov. 20, 1967).

110. *The Ecumenical Revolution: An Interpretation of the Catholic-Protestant Dialogue* (Garden City, N.Y.: Doubleday, 1969).

111. Letter from Clinchy to author, June 24, 1970.

Index